Who Should Read This Book?

We've all heard the scenario: the family on vacation stops at a road-side "dig your own" gem mine. Junior finds a sapphire the size of a peach and ends up on national television telling the world how he will spend his fortune.

𝑇 This book is for those who have read these stories and want their chance to find their own fortune. It is also a book for those who would enjoy the adventure of finding a few gems, getting them cut or polished, and making their own jewelry. It is a book for those people who want to plan a gem hunting vacation with their family. It is a book for those who study the metaphysical properties of gems and minerals and would like to add to their personal collections.

𝑇 This book is for those who would like to keep the art of rock-hounding alive and pass it on to their children. It is a book on where to find your own gems and minerals and on how to begin what for many is a lifelong hobby.

𝑇 This is a book for those who aren't interested in the "hidden treasure map through mosquito-infested no-man's-land" approach to treasure hunting but do want to find gems and minerals. It is for those who want to get out the pick and shovel and get a little dirty. (Although at some mines they bring the buckets of pre-dug dirt to you at an environmentally temperature controlled sluicing area.)

Many an unsuspecting tourist has stopped at a mine to try his or her luck and become a rockhound for life. Watch out! Your collection may end up taking the place of your car in your garage.

Good hunting!

This volume is one in a four-volume series.

VOLUME 1: **Northwest States**
Alaska
Idaho
Iowa
Minnesota
Montana
Nebraska
North Dakota
Oregon
South Dakota
Washington
Wyoming

VOLUME 2: **Southwest States**
Arizona
California
Colorado
Hawaii
Kansas
Nevada
New Mexico
Oklahoma
Texas
Utah

VOLUME 3: **Southeast States**
Alabama
Arkansas
Florida
Georgia
Kentucky
Louisiana
Mississippi
Missouri
North Carolina
South Carolina
Tennessee
Virginia
West Virginia

VOLUME 4: **Northeast States**
Connecticut
Delaware
District of Columbia
Illinois
Indiana
Maine
Maryland
Massachusetts
Michigan
New Hampshire
New Jersey
New York
Ohio
Pennsylvania
Rhode Island
Vermont
Wisconsin

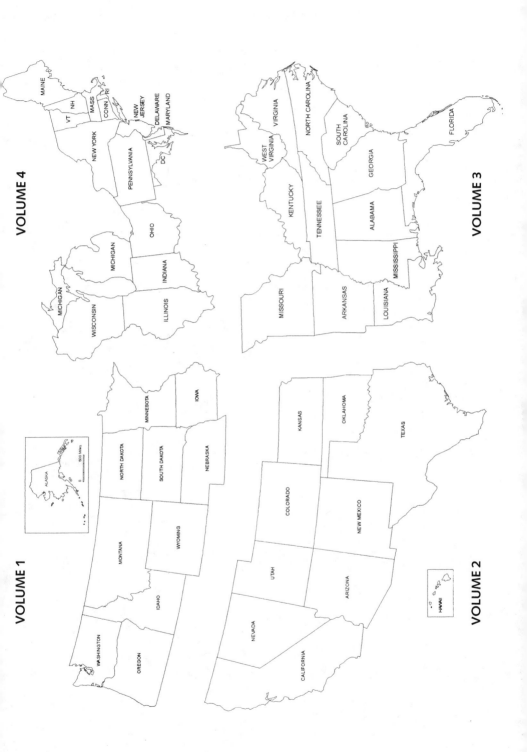

VOLUME 4

VOLUME 3

VOLUME 1

VOLUME 2

The Treasure Hunter's

GEM & MINERAL GUIDES TO THE U.S.A.

2ND EDITION

Where & How to Dig, Pan, and Mine Your Own Gems & Minerals

VOLUME 4: NORTHEAST STATES

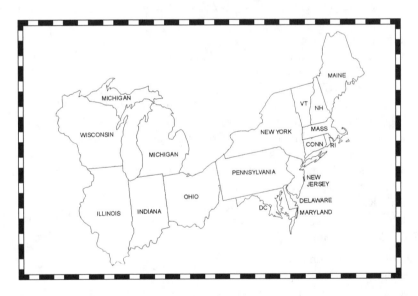

by KATHY J. RYGLE AND STEPHEN F. PEDERSEN

Preface by Antoinette Matlins, P.G.,
author of *Gem Identification Made Easy*

GEMSTONE PRESS
Woodstock, Vermont

The Treasure Hunter's Gem & Mineral Guides to the U.S.A.: 2nd Edition
Where & How to Dig, Pan, and Mine Your Own Gems & Minerals
Volume 4: Northeast States

2003 Second Edition
© 2003 by Kathy J. Rygle and Stephen F. Pedersen
Preface © 2003 by Antoinette Matlins

1999 First Edition

Library of Congress Cataloging-in-Publication Data
Rygle, Kathy J., 1955–
    Treasure hunter's gem & mineral guides to the U.S.A. : where & how to dig, pan, and mine your own gems & minerals / Kathy J. Rygle and Stephen F. Pedersen.
        p.   cm.
    Includes index.
    Contents: [1] Northwest region — [2] Southwest region — [3] Northeast region — [4] Southeast region.
      ISBN 0-943763-24-X (pbk. : NW). — ISBN 0-943763-25-8 (pbk. : SW). — ISBN 0-943763-27-4 (pbk. : NE). — ISBN 0-943763-26-6 (pbk. : SE)
    1. Minerals—United States—Collection and preservation Guidebooks.
2. Precious stones—United States—Collection and preservation Guidebooks.
3. United States Guidebooks.
    I. Pedersen, Stephen F., 1948–   . II. Title. III. Title: Treasure hunter's gem and mineral guides to the U.S.A.
QE375.R94 1999
549.973—dc21   99-39215
    Second edition data available upon request.

Cover design: Bronwen Battaglia
Text design: Chelsea Dippel

10   9   8   7   6   5   4   3   2   1

Manufactured in the United States of America

Published by GemStone Press
A Division of LongHill Partners, Inc.
Sunset Farm Offices, Route 4, P.O. Box 237
Woodstock, VT 05091
Tel: (802) 457-4000   Fax: (802) 457-4004
www.gemstonepress.com

Dedications, with love, to our parents and children:

To my parents, Joe and Helen Rygle, who taught me the love of nature; my earliest remembrances of "rockhounding" are hikes with my dad in the fields, forests, and streams near our home. I also remember weekend trips with my mother to a shop that sold specimens of minerals from around the world. To my daughter, Annie Rygle, who shares with me and continues to show me the wonders of nature. Also, thanks to Annie for helping me sort the information for the updates.   —K. J. R.

To my parents, Cliff and Leone Pedersen, who taught me to value nature and to not quit. To my daughters Kristi and Debbie, who challenge me to keep growing.   —S. F. P.

To our combined families, including Georgia Pedersen, and to family no longer with us.

With special thanks:

To all the owners of fee dig mines and guide services, curators and staff of public and private museums, mine owners, and miners. Our thanks to all those individuals both past and present who share the wonders of the earth with us.

To our agent, Barb Doyen, and her childhood rock collection.

To our publisher, Stuart M. Matlins, editor Emily Wichland, and all the staff at GemStone Press for their guidance, assistance, and patience.

To Mrs. Betty Jackson for, in her own way, telling Kathy to write the book.

To God and the wonders He has given us.

And finally, to each other, with love and the perseverance to keep on trying.

Volume 4—Northeast States

CONTENTS

Preface 11
Introduction 19
    How to Use This Guide. 21
    Equipment and Safety Precautions 25
    Mining Techniques 30
    Notes on Gem Faceting, Cabbing, and Mounting Services 35

State Listings
    Connecticut 37
    Delaware 41
    District of Columbia 44
    Illinois. 46
    Indiana 52
    Maine. 57
    Maryland 66
    Massachusetts 68
    Michigan 72
    New Hampshire 86
    New Jersey 90
    New York 99
    Ohio. 109
    Pennsylvania 116
    Rhode Island. 127
    Vermont. 129
    Wisconsin 132

Indexes
    Index by State. 137
    Index by Gems and Minerals 162

Enjoying Stones
    Annual Events 172
    State Gem and Mineral Symbols 174

Finding Your Own Birthstone 176
Finding Your Anniversary Stone 178
Finding Your Zodiac Stone 180
Some Publications on Gems and Minerals 185

Send Us Your Feedback 187

PREFACE

All-American Gems

by Antoinette Matlins, P.G.

When Americans think of costly and fabled gems, they associate them with exotic origins—Asia, South Africa or Brazil. They envision violent jungle quests or secret cellars of a sultanate, perhaps scenes from a Jorge Amado novel or from *A Thousand and One Nights,* a voluptuous Indian princess whose sari is adorned with the plentiful rubies and sapphires of her land, or a Chinese emperor sitting atop a throne flanked by dragons carved from exquisitely polished jade.

Asked what gems are mined in the United States, most Americans would probably draw a blank. We know our country is paved with one of the finest highway systems in the world, but we don't know that just below the surface, and sometimes on top of it, is a glittering pavement of gemstones that would color Old Glory. The red rubies of North Carolina, the white diamonds of Arkansas, the blue sapphires of Montana—America teems with treasures that its citizens imagine come from foreign lands. These include turquoise, tourmaline, amethyst, pearls, opals, jade, sapphires, emeralds, rubies, and even gem-quality diamonds.

Not only does America have quantity, it has quality. American gems compare very favorably with gems from other countries. In fact, fine gemstones found in the U.S. can rival specimens from anywhere else in the world. Some gems, like the luxurious emerald-green hiddenite and steely blue benitoite, are found only in America. Others, like the tourmalines of Maine and California, rival specimens found in better-known locations such as Brazil and Zambia.

The discovery of gemstones in U.S. terrain has been called a lost chapter in American history. It continues to be a saga of fashion and fable that, like the stones themselves, are a deep part of our national heritage. Appreciation of our land's generous yield of sparkling colored stones reached a zenith at the end of the nineteenth century with the art nouveau movement and its utilization of them. When the Boer Wars ended, South Africa's diamonds and platinum eclipsed many of our own then so-called semiprecious stones. Not until the 1930s, and again starting with the 1960s, did economics and the yen for color make gems more desirable again.

In the late 1800s, the nation sought out and cherished anything that was unique to the land. The search for gemstones in America coincided with the exploration of the West, and nineteenth-century mineralogists, some bonafide and others self-proclaimed, fulfilled that first call for "Made in America." Their discoveries created sensations not only throughout America but in the capitals of Europe and as far away as China. The Europeans, in fact, caught on before the Americans, exhibiting some of America's finest specimens in many of Europe's great halls.

But the search for gemstones in this country goes back even further than the nineteenth century. In 1541, the Spanish explorer Francisco Coronado trekked north from Mexico in the footsteps of Cortés and Pizarro, searching not only for gold but also for turquoise, amethyst and emeralds. In the early 1600s, when English settlers reached Virginia, they had been instructed "to searche for gold and such jeweles as ye may find."

But what eluded the Spanish explorers and early settlers was unearthed by their descendants. Benitoite, which may be our nation's most uniquely attractive gem, was discovered in 1907 in California's San Benito River headwaters. A beautiful, rare gem with the color of fine sapphire and the fire of a diamond, benitoite is currently found in gem quality only in San Benito, California.

Like many of America's finest stones discovered during the "Gem Rush" of the nineteenth century, benitoite was held in higher regard throughout the rest of the world than it was on its native U.S. soil.

The gem occurs most commonly in various shades of blue. A fine-quality blue benitoite can resemble fine blue sapphire, but it is even more brilliant. It has one weakness, however: in comparison to sapphire, it is relatively soft. It is therefore best used in pendants, brooches and earrings, or in rings with a protective setting.

While benitoite is among the rarest of our gems, our riches hardly stop there. America is the source of other unusual gems, including three even more uniquely American stones, each named after an American: kunzite, hiddenite and morganite.

The story of all-American kunzite is inseparable from the achievements of two men: Charles Lewis Tiffany, founder of Tiffany & Co., and Dr. George Frederick Kunz, world-renowned gemologist. By seeking, collecting and promoting gems found in America, these two did more for the development of native stones than anyone else during, or since, their time.

While working for Tiffany in the late 1800s, Dr. Kunz received a package in the mail containing a stone that the sender believed to be an unusual tourmaline. The stone came from an abandoned mine at Pala Mountain, California, where collectors had found traces of spodumene—a gemstone prized by the ancients but which no one had been able to find for many years. Dr. Kunz was ecstatic to find before him a specimen of "extinct spodumene of a gloriously lilac color." A fellow gemologist, Dr. Charles Baskerville, named the find "kunzite" in his honor.

Kunzite has become a favorite of such designers as Paloma Picasso, not only because of its distinctive shades—lilac, pink, and yellow-green orchid—but because it is one of a diminishing number of gems available in very large sizes at affordable prices. It is a perfect choice for the centerpiece around which to create a very bold, dramatic piece of jewelry. Designer Picasso's creations include a magnificent necklace using a 400-carat kunzite. Although it is a moderately hard stone, kunzite is easily fractured, and care must be taken to avoid any sharp blows.

Kunzite's sister gem, hiddenite, is also a truly "all-American" stone. In 1879, William Earl Hidden, an engraver and mineralogist, was sent to North Carolina on behalf of the great American inventor and prospector Thomas Alva Edison to search for platinum. Hidden found none of the precious white metal but in his pursuit unearthed a new green gemstone, which was named "hiddenite" in his honor.

Less well known than kunzite, hiddenite is an exquisite, brilliant emerald-green variety of spodumene not found anyplace else in the world. While light green and yellow-green shades have been called hiddenite, the Gemological Institute of America—this country's leading authority on gemstones—considers only the emerald-green shade of spodumene, found exclusively in the Blue Ridge Mountains of Mitchell County, North Carolina, to be true hiddenite.

The foothills of the Blue Ridge Mountains also possess America's most significant emerald deposits. While output is minimal compared to Colombia, Zambia or Pakistan, the Rist Mine in Hiddenite, North Carolina, has produced some very fine emeralds, comparable to Colombian stones. The discovery was first made by a farmer plowing his field who found them lying loose on the soil. The country folk, not knowing what they had come across, called the stones "green bolts."

In August 1970, a 26-year-old "rock hound" named Wayne Anthony found a glowing 59-carat "green bolt" at the Rist Mine only two feet from the surface. It was cut into a 13.14-carat emerald of very fine color. Tiffany & Co. later purchased the stone and called it the Carolina Emerald. "The gem is superb," said Paul E. Desautels, then the curator of mineralogy at the Smithsonian Institution. "It can stand on its own merits as a fine and lovely gem of emerald from anywhere, including Colombia." In 1973, the emerald became the official state stone of North Carolina.

A California prize, the warm peach- or pink-shaded morganite, was named by Dr. Kunz for financier John Pierpont Morgan, who purchased the Bement gem collection for donation to the American Museum of Natural History in New York, where it can be viewed today. Morganite is a member of the beryl family, which gives us aquamarine (the clear blue variety of beryl) and emerald (the deep green variety of beryl). However, morganite is available in much larger sizes than its mineralogical cousins and is much more affordable.

Many consider the core of our national treasure chest to be gems like the tourmalines of Maine and California and the sapphires of Montana, gems that are mined in commercial quantities and have earned worldwide reputations. One day in the fall of 1820, two young boys, Ezekiel Holmes and Elijah Hamlin, were rock hunting on Mount Mica in Oxford County, Maine. On the way home, one of the boys saw a flash of green light coming from underneath an uprooted tree. The find was later identified as tourmaline, and Mount Mica became the site of the first commercial gem mine in the United States. The mine was initially worked by Elijah Hamlin and his brother Hannibal, who later became Abraham Lincoln's vice president.

The colors of the rainbow meld delicately in the tourmalines of Maine, producing some of the finest specimens in the world, rivaling in quality even those from Brazil. A 150-mile strip in central Maine provides shades of apple green, burgundy red and salmon pink, to mention just a few. Some stones are bi-colored.

Miners are kept busy in the Pala district of San Diego County, California, as well. California, in fact, is North America's largest producer of gem-quality tourmaline.

The hot-pink tourmalines, for which California is famous, began to come into greater demand in 1985, as pastel-colored stones became more and more coveted by chic women around the globe. Curiously enough, over one hundred years ago the Chinese rejoiced in the fabulous colors of this fashionable stone. The Empress Dowager of the Last Chinese Imperial Dynasty sent emissaries to California in search of pink tourmalines. She garnished her robes with carved tourmaline buttons and toggles, and started a fad which overtook China. Much of the empress's collection of fine carvings was lost or stolen when the dynasty fell around 1912, but artifacts made from California's pink tourmaline can be seen today in a Beijing museum. China's fascination with pink tourmalines lasted long after the empress. In 1985, a contingent of the Chinese Geological Survey came to California with two requests: to see Disneyland and the Himalaya Mine, original site of California pink tourmaline.

While the Chinese are mesmerized by our tourmalines, Americans have always been attracted to China's jade. But perhaps we ought to take stock of our own. Wyoming, in fact, is the most important producer of the stone in the Western Hemisphere. The state produces large quantities of good-quality green nephrite jade—the type most commonly used in jewelry and carvings. California also boasts some jade, as does Alaska. Chinese immigrants panning for gold in California in the late 1800s found large boulders of nephrite and sent them back to China, where the jade was carved and sold within China and around the world.

The U.S. is also one of the largest producers of turquoise. Americans mostly associate this stone with American Indian jewelry, but its use by mainstream designers has regularly come in and out of fashion.

Some of the most prized gems of America are the stunning sapphires from Yogo Gulch, Montana. These sapphires emit a particularly pleasing shade of pale blue, and are known for their clarity and brilliance.

The Montana mine was originally owned by a gold-mining partnership. In 1895, an entire summer's work netted a total of only $700 in gold plus a cigar box full of heavy blue stones. The stones were sent to Tiffany & Co. to be identified. Tiffany then sent back a check for $3,750 for the entire box of obviously valuable stones.

Once one can conceive of gem-quality sapphires in America, it takes only a small stretch of the mind to picture the wonderful diamonds found here. A 40.23-carat white gem found in Murfreesboro, Arkansas, was cut into a 14.42-carat emerald-cut diamond named Uncle Sam. Other large diamonds include a 23.75-carat diamond found in the mid-nineteenth century in Manchester, Virginia, and a greenish 34.46-carat diamond named the Punch Jones, which was claimed to have been found in Peterstown, West Virginia.

Each year, thousands of people visit Crater of Diamonds State Park in Arkansas, where, for a fee, they can mine America's only proven location of gem-quality diamonds. Among them is a group known as "regulars" who visit the park looking for their "retirement stone."

In 1983, one of the regulars, 82-year-old Raymond Shaw, came across a 6.7-carat rough diamond. He sold it for $15,000 uncut. According to Mark Myers, assistant superintendent of the state park, the stone was cut into an exceptionally fine, 2.88-carat gem (graded E/Flawless by the Gemological Institute of America). Myers says the cut stone, later called the Shaw Diamond, was offered for sale for $58,000.

Diamonds have also been found along the shores of the Great Lakes, in many localities in California, in the Appalachian Mountains, in Illinois, Indiana, Ohio, Kentucky, New York, Idaho and Texas. Exploration for diamonds continues in Michigan, Wisconsin, Colorado and Wyoming, according to the U.S. Bureau of Mines. The discovery of gem-quality diamonds in Alaska in 1986 initiated a comprehensive search there for man's most valued gem.

Many questions concerning this country's store of gems remain unanswered. "Numerous domestic deposits of semiprecious gem stones are known and have been mined for many years," wrote the Bureau of Mines in a 1985 report. "However, no systematic evaluations of the magnitude of these deposits have been made and no positive statements can be made about them." Even as the United States continues to offer up its kaleidoscopic range of gems, our American soil may hold a still greater variety and quantity of gems yet to be unearthed.

And here, with the help of these down-to-earth (in the best possible way!)

guides, you can experience America's gem and mineral riches for yourself. In these pages rockhounds, gemologists, vacationers, and families alike will find a hands-on introduction to the fascinating world of gems and minerals . . . and a treasure map to a sparkling side of America. Happy digging!

T

Antoinette Matlins, P.G. is an internationally respected gem and jewelry expert, author and lecturer. Active in the gem trade and a popular media guest, she has been seen on ABC, CBS, NBC, and CNN, educating consumers about gems and jewelry and exposing fraud. Her books include *Jewelry & Gems: The Buying Guide; Jewelry & Gems at Auction: The Definitive Guide to Buying & Selling at the Auction House & on Internet Auction Sites; Engagement & Wedding Rings: The Definitive Buying Guide for People in Love; The Pearl Book: The Definitive Buying Guide;* and *Gem Identification Made Easy: A Hands-On Guide to More Confident Buying & Selling* (all GemStone Press).

Introduction

This is a guide to commercially operated gem and mineral mines (fee dig mines) within the United States that offer would-be treasure hunters the chance to "dig their own," from diamonds to thundereggs.

For simplicity, the term *fee dig site* is used to represent all types of fee-based mines or collection sites. However, for liability reasons, many mines no longer let collectors dig their own dirt, but rather dig it for them and provide it in buckets or bags. Some fee-based sites involve surface collection.

This book got its start when the authors, both environmental scientists, decided to make their own wedding rings. Having heard stories about digging your own gems, they decided to dig their own stones for their rings. So off to Idaho and Montana they went, taking their three children, ages 8, 13, and 15 at the time, in search of opals and garnets, their birthstones. They got a little vague information before and during the trip on where to find gem mines and in the process got lost in some of those "mosquito-infested lands." But when they did find actual "dig your own" mines (the kind outlined in this book), they found opals, garnets, and even sapphires. They have since made other trips to fee dig mines and each time have come home with treasures and some incredible memories.

The authors are also now the proud owners of a set of lapidary equipment, i.e., rock saw and rock polisher. They first used them to cut thundereggs collected from a mine in Oregon. The next project was to trim the many pounds of fossil fish rocks they acquired at a fee dig fossil site. The sequel to this guide series will cover authorized fossil collecting sites as well as museums on fossils and dinosaurs. It will include such topics as where to view and even make plaster casts of actual dinosaur tracks. There are even museums where kids of all ages can dig up a full-sized model of a dinosaur!

Types of Sites

The purpose of this book is principally to guide the reader to fee dig mine sites. These are gem or mineral mines where you hunt for the gem or mineral in ore at or from the mine. At fee dig sites where you are actually permitted to go into the field and dig for yourself, you will normally be shown what the gem or mineral you are seeking looks like in its natural state (much different from the polished or cut stone). Often someone is available to go out in the field with you and show you where to dig. At sites where you purchase gem- or mineral-bearing ore (either native or enriched) for washing in a flume, the process is the same: there will usually be examples of rough stones for comparison, and help in identifying your finds.

Also included are a few areas that are not fee dig sites but that are well-defined collecting sites, usually parks or beaches.

Guided field trips are a little different. Here the guide may or may not have examples of what you are looking for, but he or she will be with you in the field to help in identifying finds.

For the more experienced collector, there are field collecting areas where you are on your own in identifying what you have found. Several fee areas and guided field trips appropriate for the experienced collector are available. Check out the listings for Ruggles Mine (Grafton, NH); Harding Mine (Dixon, NM); Poland Mining Camps (Poland, ME); Perhams (West Paris, ME); and Gem Mountain Quarry Trips (Spruce Pine, NC).

Knowing What You're Looking For

Before you go out into the field, it is a good idea to know what you are looking for. Most of the fee dig mines listed in this guide will show you specimens before you set out to find your own. If you are using a guide service, you have the added bonus of having a knowledgeable person with you while you search to help you find the best place to look and help you identify your finds.

Included here is a listing of museums that contain rock and gem exhibits. A visit to these museums will help prepare you for your search. You may find examples of gems in the rough and examples of mineral specimens similar to the ones you will be looking for. Museums will most likely have displays of gems or minerals native to the local area. Some of the gems and minerals listed in this guide are of significant interest, and specimens of them can be found in museums around the country. Displays accompanying the exhibits might tell you how the gems and minerals were found, and their place in our nation's history. Many museums also hold collecting field trips or geology programs, or may be able to put you in touch with local rock and lapidary clubs.

For more information on learning how to identify your finds yourself—and even how to put together a basic portable "lab" to use at the sites—the book *Gem Identification Made Easy* by Antoinette Matlins and A. C. Bonanno (GemStone Press) is a good resource.

Rock shops are another excellent place to view gem and mineral specimens before going out to dig your own. A listing of rock shops would be too extensive to include in a book such as this. A good place to get information on rock shops in the area you plan to visit is to contact the chamber of commerce for that area. Rock shops may be able to provide information not only on rockhounding field trips but also on local rock clubs that sponsor trips.

Through mine tours you can see how minerals and gems were and are taken from the earth. On these tours, visitors learn what miners go through to remove the ores from the earth. This will give you a better appreciation for those sparkly gems you see in the showroom windows, and for many of the items we all take for granted in daily use.

You will meet other rockhounds at the mine. Attending one of the yearly events listed in the guide will also give you the chance to meet people who share your interest in gems and minerals and exchange ideas, stories, and knowledge of the hobby.

How to Use This Guide

To use this book, you can pick a state and determine what mining is available there, or pick a gem or mineral and determine where to go to "mine" it.

In this guide are indexes that will make the guide simple to use. If you are interested in finding a particular gem or mineral, go to the Index by Gem or Mineral in the back of the book. In this index, gems and minerals are listed in alphabetical order with the states and cities where fee dig sites for that gem or mineral may be found.

If you are interested in learning of sites near where you live, or in the area where you are planning a vacation, or if you simply want to know whether there are gems and minerals in a particular location, go to the Index by State, located in the back of the guide. The state index entries are broken down into three categories: Fee Dig Sites/Guide Services, Museums and Mine Tours, and Special Events and Tourist Information.

There are also several special indexes for use in finding your birthstone, anniversary stone, or zodiac stone.

Site Listings

The first section of each chapter lists fee dig sites and guide services that are available in each state. Included with the location of each site is a description of the site, directions to find it, what equipment is provided, and what you must supply. Costs are listed, along with specific policies of the site. Also included are other services available at the site and information on camping, lodging, etc. in the area of the site. Included in the section with fee dig sites are guide services for collecting gems and minerals.

In the second section of each chapter, museums of special interest to the gem/mineral collector and mine tours available to the public are listed. Besides being wonderful ways to learn about earth science, geology, and mining history (many museums and tours also offer child-friendly exhibits), museums are particularly useful for viewing gems and minerals in their rough or natural state before going out in the field to search for them.

The third section of each chapter lists special events involving gems and minerals, and resources for general tourist information.

A sample of the listings for fee dig mines and guide services (Section 1 in the guides) is on the next page.

Tips for mining:

1. Learn what gems or minerals can be found at the mine you are going to visit.
2. Know what the gem or mineral that you're hunting looks like in the rough before you begin mining.

Visiting local rock shops and museums will help in this effort.
3. When in doubt, save any stone that you are unsure about. Have an expert at the mine or at a local rock shop help you identify your find.

Sample Fee Dig Site Listing

TOWN in which the site is located / *Native or enriched[1]* • *Easy, moderate, difficult[2]*

Dig your own *T*

The following gems may be found:
• List of gems and minerals found at the mine

Mine name
Owner or contact (where available)
Address
Phone number
Fax
E-mail address
Website address

Open: Months, hours, days
Info: Descriptive text regarding the site, including whether equipment is provided
Admission: Fee to dig; costs for predug dirt
Other services available
Other area attractions (at times)
Information on lodging or campground facilities (where available)
Directions

Map (where available)

Notes:

1. Native or enriched. *Native* refers to gems or minerals found in the ground at the site, put there by nature. *Enriched* means that gems and minerals from an outside source have been brought in and added to the soil. Enriching is also called "salting"—it is a guaranteed return. Whatever is added in a salted mine is generally the product of some commercial mine elsewhere. Thus, it is an opportunity to "find" gemstones from around the world the easy way, instead of traveling to jungles and climbing mountains in remote areas of the globe. Salted mines are particularly nice for giving children the opportunity to find a wide variety of gems and become involved in gem identification. The authors have tried to indicate if a mine is enriched, but to be sure, ask at the mine beforehand. If the status could not be determined, this designation was left out.

2. Sites are designated as easy, moderate, or difficult. This was done to give you a feel for what a site may be like. You should contact the site and make a determination for yourself if you have any doubts.

Easy: This might be a site where the gem hunter simply purchases bags or buckets of predug dirt, washes the ore in a flume or screens the gem-bearing gravel to concentrate the gems, and flips the screen. The gems or minerals are then picked out of the material remaining in the screen. A mine which has set aside a pile of mine material for people to pick through would be another type of site designated as "Easy."

Moderate: Mining at a "Moderate" site might mean digging with a shovel, then loading the dirt into buckets, followed by sifting and sluicing. Depending on your knowledge of mineral identification, work at a "Moderate" site might include searching the surface of the ground at an unsupervised area for a gem or mineral you are not familiar with (this could also be considered difficult).

Difficult: This might be a site requiring tools such as picks and shovels, or sledgehammers and chisels. The site may be out of the way and/or difficult to get to. Mining might involve heavy digging with the pick and shovel or breaking gems or minerals out of base rock using a sledge or chisel.

Special Note:

Although most museums and many fee dig sites are handicapped accessible, please check with the listing directly.

Maps

Maps are included to help you locate the sites in the guide. At the beginning of each state, there is a state map showing the general location of towns where sites are located.

Local maps are included in a listing when the information was available. *These maps are not drawn to scale!* These maps provide information to help you get to the site but are not intended to be a substitute for a road map. Please check directly with the site you are interested in for more detailed directions.

Fees
Fees listed in these guides were obtained when the book was updated, and may have changed. They are included to give you at least a general idea of the costs you will be dealing with. Please contact the site directly to confirm charges.

Many museums have discounts for members and for groups, as well as special programs for school groups. Please check directly with the institution for information. Many smaller and/or private institutions have no fee, but do appreciate donations to help meet the costs of staying open.

Many sites accept credit cards; some may not. Please check ahead for payment options if this is important.

Requesting Information by Mail
When requesting information by mail, it is always appreciated if you send a SASE (self-addressed stamped envelope) along with your request. Doing this will often speed up the return of information.

Equipment and Safety Precautions

Equipment
The individual sites listed in these guides often provide equipment at the mine. Please note that some fee dig sites place limitations on the equipment you can use at their site. Those limitations will be noted where the information was available. Always abide by the limitations; remember that you are a guest at the site.

On the following pages are figures showing equipment for rockhounding. Figures A and B identify some of the equipment you may be told you need at a site. Figure C shows material needed to collect, package, transport, and record your findings. Figure D illustrates typical safety equipment.

Always use safety glasses with side shields or goggles when you are hammering or chiseling. Chips of rock or metal from your tools can fly off at great speed in any direction when hammering. Use gloves to protect your hands as well.

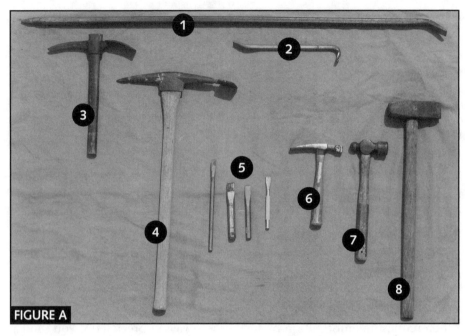

FIGURE A

1. Crowbar
2. Pry bar
3. Smaller pick
4. Rock pick
5. Various-sized chisels (*Note:* When working with a hammer and chisel, you may want to use a chisel holder, not shown, for protecting your hand if you miss. Always use eye protection with side shields and gloves!)
6. Rock hammer (*Note:* Always use eye protection.)
7. 3-pound hammer (*Note:* Always use eye protection.)
8. Sledgehammer (*Note:* When working with a sledgehammer, wear hard-toed boots along with eye protection.)

Other useful tools not shown include an ultraviolet hand lamp, and a hand magnifier.

Not pictured, but something you don't want to forget, is your camera and plenty of extra film. You may also want to bring along your video camera to record that "big" find, no matter what it might be.

Not pictured, but to be considered: knee pads and seat cushions.

Other Safety Precautions

- Never go into the field or on an unsupervised site alone. With protective clothing, reasonable care, proper use of equipment, and common sense,

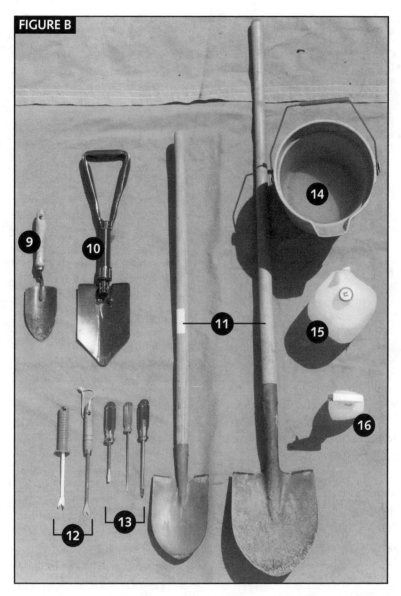

FIGURE B

9. Garden trowel
10. Camp shovel
11. Shovels
12. Garden cultivators
13. Screwdrivers

14. Bucket of water
15. (Plastic) jug of water
16. Squirt bottle of water; comes in handy at many of the mines to wash off rocks so you can see if they are or contain gem material

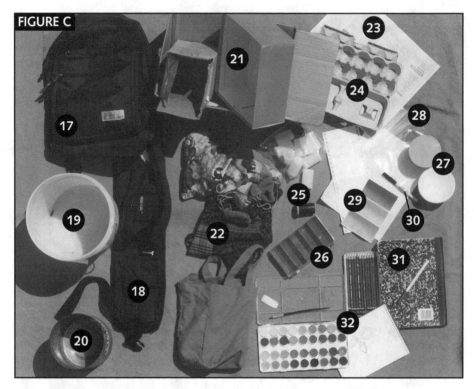

FIGURE C

17. Backpack
18. Waist pack to hold specimens
19. Bucket to hold specimens
20. Coffee can to hold specimens
21. Boxes to pack, transport, and ship specimens
22. Bags—various sized bags to carry collected specimens in the field
23. Newspaper to wrap specimens for transport
24. Egg cartons to transport delicate specimens
25. Empty film canisters to hold small specimens
26. Plastic box with dividers to hold small specimens
27. Margarine containers to hold small specimens

28. Reclosable plastic bags to hold small specimens
29. Gummed labels to label specimens (Whether you are at a fee dig site or with a guide, usually there will be someone to help you identify your find. It is a good idea to label the find when it is identified so that when you reach home, you won't have boxes of unknown rocks.)
30. Waterproof marker for labeling
31. Field log book to make notes on where specimens were found
32. Sketching pencils, sketchbook, paint to record your finds and the surrounding scenery

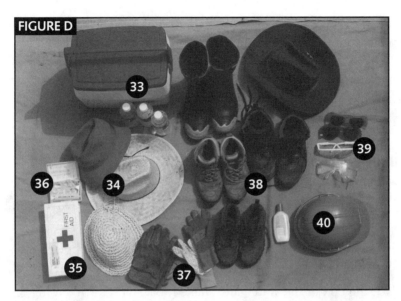

FIGURE D

33. Food and water—always carry plenty of drinking water (*Note:* many sites tell you in advance if they have food and water available or if you should bring some; however, it is always a good idea to bring extra drinking water. Remember—if you bring it in, pack it back out.)

34. Hats. Many of the sites are in the open, and the summer sun can be hot and dangerous to unprotected skin. Check with the site to see if they have any recommendations for protective clothing. Also, don't forget sunscreen.

35. First aid/safety kit

36. Snakebite kit. If the area is known to have snakes, be alert and take appropriate safety measures, such as boots and long pants. (*Note:* while planning our first gem-hunting trip, we read that the first aid kit should contain a snakebite kit. Just like rockhounds, snakes seem to love rocky areas!) In most cases, if you visit sites in the book, you will be either at a flume provided by the facility, or with an experienced guide. At the first, you will most likely never see a snake; at the second, your guide will fill you in on precautions. For listings where you will be searching on a ranch or state park, ask about special safety concerns such as snakes and insects when you pay your fee. These sites may not be for everyone.

37. Gloves to protect your hands when you are working with sharp rock or using a hammer or chisel

38. Boots—particularly important at sites where you will be doing a lot of walking, or walking on rocks

39. Safety glasses with side shields, or goggles. Particularly important at hard rock sites or any site where you or others may be hitting rocks. Safety glasses are available with tinted lenses for protection from the sun.

40. Hard hats—may be mandatory if you are visiting an active quarry or mine; suggested near cliffs

accidents should be avoided, but in the event of an illness or accident, you always want to have someone with you who can administer first aid and call for or seek help.

- Always keep children under your supervision.
- Never enter old abandoned mines or underground diggings!
- Never break or hammer rocks close to another person!

Mining Techniques

How to Sluice for Gems

This is the most common technique used at fee dig mines where you buy a bucket of gem ore (gem dirt) and wash it at a flume.

1. Place a quantity of the gem ore in the screen box, and place the screen box in the water. Use enough gem ore to fill the box about a third.

2. Place the box in the water, and shake it back and forth, raising one side,

Clockwise from top: Gold pan; screen box used for sluicing; screen box used for screening.

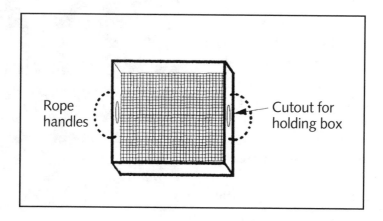

Rope handles

Cutout for holding box

How to Build a Screen Box

1. A screen box that is easy to handle is generally built from 1" x 4" lumber and window screening.

2. Decide on the dimensions of the screen box you want, and cut the wood accordingly. Dimensions generally run from 12" x 12" up to 18" x 18". Remember that the end pieces will overlap the side pieces, so cut the end pieces 1½" longer.

3. There are two alternative methods of construction. In one, drill pilot holes in the end pieces, and use wood screws to fasten the end pieces to the side pieces. In the other, use angle irons and screws to attach the ends and sides.

4. Cut the screening to be ¼" smaller than the outside dimensions of the screen box, and use staples to attach the screen to the bottom of the box. Use metal screening rather than plastic if possible. For a stronger box, cut ¼" or ⅜" hardware cloth to the same dimensions as the screening, and staple the hardware cloth over the screening. The hardware cloth will provide support for the screening.

5. Cut ¼" wood trim to fit, and attach it to the bottom of the box to cover the edges of the screening and hardware cloth and staples.

6. If you like, add rope handles or cut handholds in the side pieces for easier handling.

then the other, so that the material in the box moves back and forth. What you are doing is making the stones move around in the screen box, while washing dirt and sand out of the mixture.

3. After a minute or two of washing, take the screen box out of the flume, and let it drain. Look through the stones remaining in the screen box for your treasure. If you're not sure about something, ask one of the attendants.

4. When you can't finding anything more, put the box back in the flume and wash it some more, then take it out and search again.

5. If possible, move your screen box into bright light while you are searching, since the gems and minerals often show up better in bright light.

How to Screen for Gems

This is another common technique used at fee dig mines where you buy a bucket of gem ore and screen it for gems. (The authors used this technique for garnets and sapphires in Montana.)

1. Place a quantity of the gem ore in the screen box, and place the screen box in the water. Use enough gem dirt to fill the box about a third.

2. Place the box in the water, and begin tipping it back and forth, raising one side, then the other, so that the material in the box moves back and forth. What you are doing is making the gemstones, which are heavier than the rock and dirt, move into the bottom center of the screen box while at the same time washing dirt and sand out of the mixture.

3. After a minute or two, change the direction of movement to front and back.

4. Repeat these two movements (Steps 2 and 3) three or four times.

5. Take the box out of the water and let it drain, then place a board on top and carefully flip the box over onto the sorting table. It may be helpful to

put a foam pad in the box, then put the board over it. This helps keep the stones in place when you flip the box. If you have done it right, the gemstones will be found in the center of the rocks dumped onto the board. Use tweezers to pick the rough gemstones out of the rocks, and place them in a small container.

How to Pan for Gold

The technique for panning for gold is based on the fact that gold is much heavier than rock or soil. Gently washing and swirling the gold-bearing soil in a pan causes the gold to settle to the bottom of the pan. A gold pan has a flat bottom and gently slanting sides. Some modern pans also have small ridges or rings around the inside of the pan on these slanting sides. As the soil is washed out of the pan, the gold will slide down the sides, or be caught on the ridges and stay in the pan. Here's how:

1. Begin by filling the pan with ore, about ⅔ to ¾ full.

2. Put your pan in the water, let it gently fill with water, then put the pan under the water surface. Leave the pan in the water, and mix the dirt around in the pan, cleaning and removing any large rocks.

3. Lift the pan out of the water, then gently shake the pan from side to side while swirling it at the same time. Do this for 20–30 seconds to get the gold settled to the bottom of the pan.

4. Still holding the pan out of the water, continue these motions while tilting the pan so that the dirt begins to wash out. Keep the angle of the pan so that the crease (where the bottom and sides meet) is the lowest point.

5. When there is only about a tablespoon of material left in the pan, put about ½ inch of water in the pan, and swirl the water over the remaining material. As the top material is moved off, you should see gold underneath.

6. No luck? Try again at a different spot.

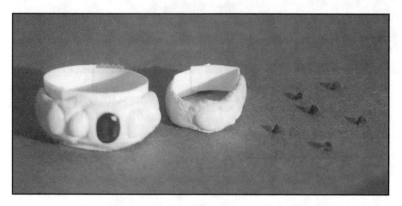

The authors sent their rough gems away for faceting. Using the faceted gems, they made crude mock-ups and sketches of the rings they wanted; then they sent the mock-ups, sketches, and gems to be made into rings.

The finished rings.

Notes on Gem Faceting, Cabbing, and Mounting Services

Many of the fee dig sites offer services to cut and mount your finds. Quality and costs vary. Trade journals such as *Lapidary Journal* and *Rock & Gem* (available at most large bookstores or by subscription) list suppliers of these services, both in the United States and overseas. Again, quality and cost vary. Local rock and gem shops in your area may offer these services, or it may be possible to work with a local jeweler. Your local rock club may be able to provide these services or make recommendations.

After their first gem-hunting trip, the authors had some of their finds faceted and cabochoned. They then designed rings and had them made using these stones, as shown in the photos on the previous page.

Taking sifted gravel to the jig at a sapphire mine in Montana. Pictured from left to right: Steve, Kathy, Annie Rygle, Debra Pedersen, Kristin Pedersen.

CONNECTICUT

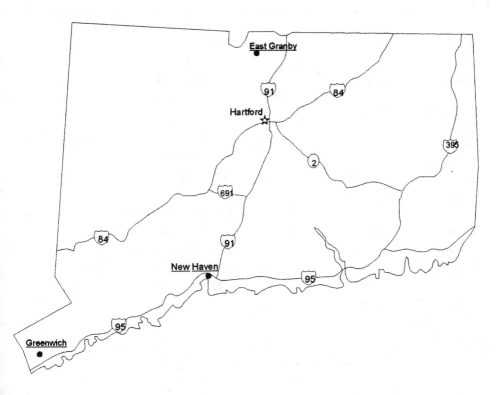

State Gemstone: Garnet (1977)

SECTION 1: Fee Dig Sites and Guide Services

No information available.

SECTION 2: Museums and Mine Tours

EAST GRANBY

Mine Tour/Museum

Old New-Gate Prison and
Copper Mine
Newgate Road
East Granby, CT 06026
Phone: (860) 653-3563
Off-season: (860) 566-3005

Open: Mid-May–October, 10:00 A.M.–
4:30 P.M., Wednesday–Sunday.
Info: The Old New-Gate Prison and
Copper Mine, formerly the Simsbury
Copper Mine, was the first American
copper mine, chartered in 1707. Ore
from the Simsbury Copper Mine aver-
aged about 12% copper and in some
cases ran as high as 50% copper. By
1773, work at the mine had nearly
ceased because of several factors, including the expense of shipping ore to England for smelting.

In December 1773, the mine became
a prison. Other copper mines existed
near New-Gate, one of which was the
Higley Mine. Between 1729 and 1737,
Dr. Samuel Higley designed the first
copper coins used for trading purposes
in the country.

A guided walking tour of the mine is
available. Because of the narrow tunnels
and low ceilings, visitors are guided in
small groups. When in the mine tunnels,
be aware that the ceilings are sometimes
low. The temperature stays in the low-
50s, and a sweater is recommended,
along with good walking shoes.
Admission: Adults $4.00, seniors $3.00,
children (6–12) $2.00. Special arrange-

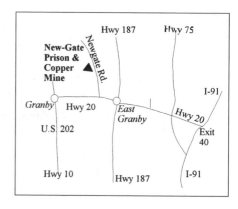

ments for groups, by appointment only. **Other services available:** Picnic area, gift shop.

Directions: From exit 40 on I-91, take Route 20W through East Granby Center to traffic light at Newgate Road. Turn right on Newgate, and drive 1 mile to mine. From Routes 10/202, take Route 20E from Granby Center for 2.8 miles to the light at Newgate Road in East Granby. Turn left on Newgate, and drive 1 mile to the mine.

GREENWICH

Museum

Bruce Museum of Arts and Sciences
One Museum Drive
Greenwich, CT 06830-7100
Phone: (203) 869-0376
Fax: (203) 869-0963
www.brucemuseum.org

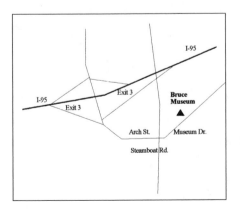

Open: All year, 10:00 A.M.–5:00 P.M., Tuesday–Sunday. Closed Monday.

Info: Exhibits of minerals and rocks are on display.

Admission: Adults $5.00, seniors and children (5–12) $4.00. On Tuesdays, admission is free.

Directions: Take exit 3 off I-95. At the end of the ramp, turn east on Arch Street, and drive to the intersection with Steamboat Road. Go straight across to Museum Drive, and the museum will be 500 feet on the left.

NEW HAVEN

Museum

Peabody Museum of Natural History
Yale University
P.O. Box 208118
170 Whitney Avenue
New Haven, CT 06520
Phone: (203) 432-5050
www.peabody.yale.edu

Open: All year except major holidays, 10:00 A.M.–5:00 P.M. Monday–Saturday, 12:00–5:00 P.M. Sunday. Groups must register in advance.

Info: Exhibits on minerals of New England and minerals of the world.

Admission: Adults $5.00, seniors over 65 and children (3–15) $3.00.

Directions: For directions, call (203) 432-5050.

SECTION 3: Special Events and Tourist Information

TOURIST INFORMATION

State Tourist Agency

Connecticut Office of Tourism
505 Hudson Street
Hartford, CT 06106
Phone: (800) CTBOUND or
(800) 282-6863
Fax: (860) 270-8077
www.ctbound.org

DELAWARE

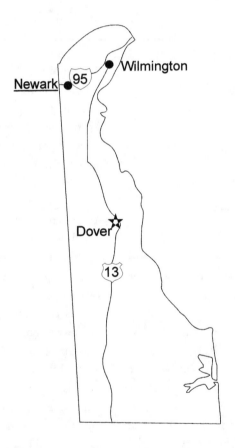

State Mineral: Sillimanite

SECTION 1: Fee Dig Sites and Guide Services

No information available.

SECTION 2: Museums and Mine Tours

NEWARK

Museum

Iron Hill Museum
1355 Old Baltimore Pike
Newark, DE 19702
Phone: (302) 368-5703
E-mail: ironhill@magpage.com

Open: All year, noon– 4:00 P.M. Wednesday–Friday. 10:00 A.M.– 4:00 P.M. Saturday. Groups of 10 or more can be booked any day of the week.

Info: The Iron Hill Museum specializes in the natural history of Delaware. The rock and mineral collection includes many Delaware specimens as well as a portion of the Irenee du Pont collection, which was donated many years ago. (The remainder of this collection is at Perry Hall on the University of Delaware Campus. This display is also open to the public.)

The museum also has an excellent display of fluorescent minerals (not from Delaware). Group programs and school field trips include a walk to the old iron mines and sometimes rock collection at the top of Iron Hill and at other sites.

The Iron Mountain area was mined for iron ore for approximately 200 years. An original open-pit iron mine exists along the museum trail, as well as spoils piles resulting from mining activity.

Before iron ore was mined, large outcrops of jasper at the site brought Native Americans to the area in search of this valuable stone (lithic) resource for making the tools necessary for survival. Evidence gathered as a result of archeological excavation indicates that the site was used as both a procurement area and a workshop complex, since both finished projectile points and late-stage rejected stone material have been recovered. Jasper, along with chert and chalcedony, is restricted to a small region called the Delaware Chalcedony Complex. Iron Hill was the only jasper source in the area and was geographically the southernmost point of access for this important resource.

Admission: Call for fees.

Directions: Call for directions.

Info: For information on other Native American stone quarries, see listings in

Calumet and Copper Harbor, MI: copper (Vol. 4); Pipestone, MN: pipestone quarries (Vol.1); Hopewell and Brownsville, OH: flint quarries (Vol. 4); and Fritch, TX: flint quarries (Vol. 2).

NEWARK

Museum

University of Delaware
Mineralogical Museum
Penny Hall
Academy Street
Newark, DE 19716-2544
Phone: (302) 831-8242
Fax: (302) 831-8251
www.udel.edu/geology.html

Open: Noon– 4:00 P.M. Tuesday–Thursday; 1:00 – 4:00 P.M. Saturday and Sunday. Closed University holidays.
Info: The museum's collection includes approximately 5,000 specimens, about 1,000 of which are on display in the Irenee du Pont Memorial Room in Penny Hall. The collection of the late Irenee du Pont forms the core of the University Mineralogical Museum. Mr. du Pont had been interested in minerals for several years and in 1919 purchased the mineral collection assembled by George Kunz, which Tiffany & Co. had on display in its Fifth Avenue showroom in New York City.

Among the specimens are crystals of gem minerals. The collection has been expanded by other donors. Mrs. David Craven, a niece of Irenee du Pont, became interested in the collection and donated funds to increase the collection and expand the Mineral Room.
Admission: Free.
Directions: In Penny Hall on the university campus.

SECTION 3: Special Events and Tourist Information

TOURIST INFORMATION

State Tourist Agency

Delaware Tourism Office
99 Kings Highway
P.O. Box 1401
Wilmington, DE 19901

Phone: (302) 739-4271;
(866) 284-7483
F ax: (302) 739-5749
www.visitdelaware.net

DISTRICT OF COLUMBIA

No information available.

Museum

Smithsonian Institution
National Museum of Natural History
10th Street and Constitution Avenue NW
Washington, D.C. 20560-0119
Phone: (202) 357-2700
www.si.edu

Open: All year, 9:00 A.M.–5:00 P.M. 7 days/week. Closed December 25.
Info: The Hall of Gems and Minerals explains mineral formation and classification. The collection includes both cut and uncut stones, including many world-famous gems. The more impressive items are housed in individual cases. Many gems and minerals from locales listed in this book are a part of the Smithsonian collection.

The National Gem and Mineral Collection contains over 375,000 individual specimens, including the Hope Diamond and the Star of Asia Sapphire. It also contains a research mineral collection used by scientists all over the world. The National Meteorite Collection is one of the three largest meteorite collections in the world, consisting of over 4,000 specimens. The National Rock and Ore Collection contains over 235,000 specimens.
Admission: Free.
Directions: Located at the corner of 10th Street and Constitution Avenue; reachable by Metro.

SECTION 3: Special Events and Tourist Information

TOURIST INFORMATION

State Tourist Agency

Washington, D.C. Convention and
Tourism Corporation
1212 New York Avenue NW, Suite 600
Washington, DC 20005
Phone: (202) 789-7000
Fax: (202) 789-7037
www.washington.org

ILLINOIS

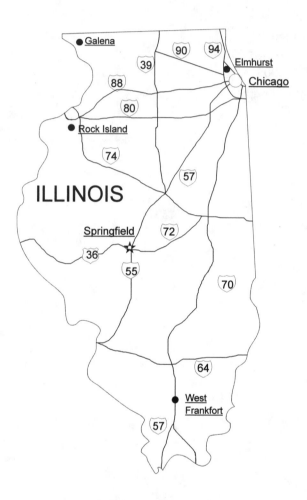

State Mineral: Fluorite

SECTION 1: Fee Dig Sites and Guide Services

No information available.

SECTION 2: Museums and Mine Tours

CHICAGO

Museum 🏛

The Field Museum
1400 S. Lake Shore Drive
Chicago, IL 60605-2496
Phone: (312) 922-9410
www.fieldmuseum.org

Open: All year, except Christmas and New Year's Day, 9:00 A.M.–5:00 P.M. 7 days/week.

Info: The gem exhibit of the Field Museum contains over 500 pieces. Displayed are the best of the Museum's 92-year-old gem collection. Most of this collection dates back to the 1893 World Exposition, when Harlow Higinbotham, a museum trustee, purchased the collection from Tiffany & Co., which had exhibited the gems during the exposition.

Visitors can learn what gems are, where they come from, and how they are used by people. Information is provided on the methods, techniques, and terminology of the gem industry, along with the superstition and lore of gemstones. The exhibit is divided into 12 sections, each devoted to a different grouping of gems, including Quartz, Cryptocrystalline Quartz, Precious Stones, Lapidary Art, Gems from Animals and Plants, Royal Gems, Diamond Replicas, Unusual Gems, Decorative Minerals, Myth and Magic, Stars and Eyes, and What Is a Gem?

Admission: Adults $8.00, children (3–11), seniors and students $4.00. Basic admission is free on Monday and Tuesday from January–February and from September 23–December 24.

Directions: Roosevelt Road at Lakeshore Drive in downtown Chicago.

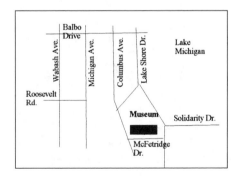

ELMHURST

Museum

Lizzadro Museum of Lapidary Art
Wilder Park
220 Cottage Hill
Elmhurst, IL 60126
Phone: (630) 833-1616

Open: All year, 10:00 A.M.–5:00 P.M. Tuesday–Saturday, 1:00–5:00 P.M. Sunday. Closed Monday. Groups should call for reservations.

Info: Joseph F. Lizzadro, Sr., gained a first-hand appreciation for the unique characteristics of the mineral world through working with rough gem material as a hobbyist and collector. The museum opened on November 4, 1962, with this statement of purpose by the Lizzadro family: "To share with others our enjoyment of the eternal beauty in gemstones and promote the study of earth science."

The museum displays over 1,300 pieces of cut and polished gems and minerals. Displays include masterpieces of lapidary work from European countries, including Germany and Italy. Fine Chinese jadeite carvings are also displayed. Visitors can see fluorescent rocks, a birthstone display, fossils, unusual or noteworthy rocks, meteorites, and micromounts.

Admission: Adults $4.00, seniors $3.00, students and teens $2.00, children 7–12 $1.00, children under 7 free. Admission free on Fridays.

Other services available: Gift shop, slide lecture programs, video programs on select Saturdays. Every Sunday afternoon a 50-minute video is shown which discusses how to start a mineral collection, where to search for specimens, and how to cut and polish stones.

Directions: Take St. Charles Road east from Highway 83 in Elmhurst. Turn left on Prospect to the Wilder Park entrance. An alternative route is to take York Avenue to Church Street, and turn west on Church to Prospect and turn right to Wilder Park.

GALENA

Mine Tour

Vinegar Hill Lead Mine and Museum
8885 N. Three Pines Road
Galena, IL 61036
Phone: (815) 777-0855

Open: June–August every day; May, September, October weekends only, 9:00

A.M.–5:00 P.M. Call for group reservations. **Info:** Galena, 6 miles south of the mine and museum, was once the lead mining capital of the world. In the mid-1850s, the Galena mines produced a total of 55,000,000 pounds of lead ore in one year. Today, the Vinegar Hill Mine is the only lead mine in Illinois open for tours. In 1798, all sections of the Furlong family fought in the battle of Vinegar Hill (in Wexford County, Ireland) in the rebellion against the British garrison. John Furlong was captured at this battle. He was sent to Canada along with many other Irish soldiers. When they heard of Julien Dubuque and his lead excursions, they deserted the British, came to the east banks of the Mississippi, and started to mine for Galena lead ore. In 1824, Furlong and three of his friends struck a rich vein of ore at Cave Branch, which is now known as Vinegar Hill.

Furlong's grandson John worked this mine in 1882, and his great-grandson Thomas worked this mine in 1934. This mine was opened for tourists by Furlong's great-great-grandson Earl in 1967 and was continued by his great-great-great-grandson Mark in 1986.

A guided tour of the old Vinegar Hill Lead Mine includes a walk down into the mine. The museum features a wide variety of lead and ore samples, along with mining tools.

Admission: Adult $5.00, students $2.50, children 5 years and under free.

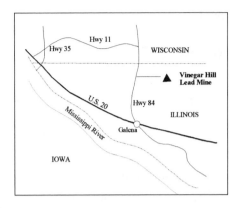

Directions: Located 6 miles north of Galena on Illinois Highway 84.

ROCK ISLAND

Museum

Augustana Fryxell Geology Museum
Augustana College
38th Street
Rock Island, IL 61201
Phone: (309) 794-7318
Fax: (309) 794-7564
www.augustana.edu/academ/geology

Open: During the academic school year, 8:00 A.M.– 4:30 P.M. Monday–Friday.

Info: The Fryxell Museum has become one of the largest and finest rock and mineral collections in the Midwest.

Admission: Free.

Directions: Located in the Swenson Hall of Geosciences on the Augustana College campus, on 38th Street in Rock Island.

ROSICLARE

Museum

The American Fluorite Museum
Main Street
P.O. Box 755
Rosiclare, IL 62982
Phone: (618) 285-3513
www.keminerals.com/american.htm

Open: March–December 1:00–4:00 P.M.
Thursday, Friday, Sunday, 10:00 A.M.–
4:00 P.M. Saturday.

Info: The museum is located in the former Rosiclare Lead and Fluorspar Mining Company office building. Displays tell the story of the fluorspar mining industry using ore specimens, mining equipment, and photographs. There is also a display of mineral specimens, including many fluorite specimens.

Admission: Adults $3.00, children 6–12 $1.00.

Directions: Call for directions.

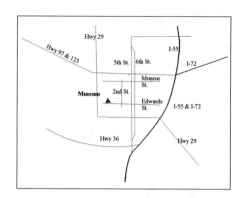

Info: Rock collections at the museum contain representative samples of most rock types, including the major formations in Illinois. Find your birthstone, touch one of the largest masses of copper, and see minerals fluoresce under ultraviolet light.

Admission: Free.

Other services available: Gift shop.

Directions: The museum is located on the southwest corner of the State Capitol grounds, at the intersection of Spring and Edwards Streets. Free parking is available nearby.

SPRINGFIELD

Museum

Illinois State Museum
Spring and Edwards Streets
Springfield, IL 62706
Phone: (217) 782-7387
www.museum.state.il.us

Open: All year, 8:30 A.M.–5:00 P.M. 6 days/week, noon–5:00 P.M. Sunday; closed on major holidays.

WEST FRANKFORT

Mine Tour

The National Coal Museum Mine 25
P.O. Box 369
Logan Road
West Frankfort, IL 62896
Phone: (618) YES-COAL; (618) 937-2625
www.coalmuseum.com

Open: March 1–December 31, 10:00 A.M.–5:00 P.M. (tours every hour) Tuesday–Sunday. Closed Thanksgiving, Christmas, and New Year's Day.

Info: The only shaft coal mine in the nation that is open to the public. During the 1-hour tour, guides take you 600 feet below ground into a real coal mine. Visitors are also able to tour 415 acres of surface facilities of this underground mine and see everything from reclamation and coal prep to environmental remediation and the shipping of mine products to market.

At the company store, visitors can view and purchase artifacts and other materials relevant to the coal mining industry.

Admission: Adults $10.00, seniors (65+) and children 7–15 $8.00, retired miner $7.00. Group rates available—call

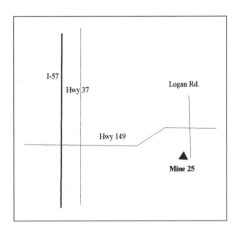

for reservations.

Directions: Exit 65 on I-57 at West Frankfort. From I-57, travel east on Highway 149 approximately 6 miles to Logan Road. Turn right and travel 1 mile to Mine 25.

SECTION 3: Special Events and Tourist Information

TOURIST INFORMATION

State Tourist Agency

Illinois Bureau of Tourism
Department of Commerce and Community Affairs
100 West Randolph Street
Suite 3–400
Chicago, IL 60601
Phone: (800) TO CONNECT or
(800) 226-6632
www.enjoyillinois.com

INDIANA

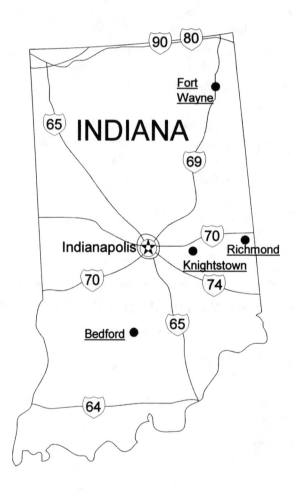

State Stone/Rock: Limestone

SECTION 1: Fee Dig Sites and Guide Services

KNIGHTSTOWN / *Native* ·
Moderate

Midwestern Gold Prospecting *T*

The following gems or minerals may be found:

- Gold

Yogi Bear's Jellystone Park
Camping Resort
Knightstown, IN 46148
Phone: (800) IGO-YOGI or
(800) 446-9644

Open: Call for information on operating hours.

Info: Pan, sluice, or dredge in a creek bed, or glacial sand and gravel deposits. The resort also has special weekend events such as Old Prospectors Weekend in May and Gold Rush Weekend in October.

Fee: If camping, adults $3.00, children $2.00. If not camping, adults $6.00, children $2.00.

Other services available: Camping cabins; fishing; camping store; showers; playground; swimming pool; paddleboats.

Directions: State Highway 109 and Interstate 70 (exit 115), 25 miles east of Indianapolis, at Knightstown.

SECTION 2: Museums and Mine Tours

BEDFORD

Museum

Land of Limestone Exhibit
Bedford Campus-Oakland City
University
405 I Street
Bedford, IN 46204
www.limestonecountry.com

For information, write:
Lawrence County Tourism Commission
and Convention Service
P.O. Box 1193, 1131 16th Street

Bedford, IN 47421
Phone: (812) 275-7637; (800) 798-0769

Open: All year, Monday–Friday 8:00 A.M.–5:00 P.M., Saturday 9:00 A.M.– noon.
Info: Limestone has been quarried in this part of southern Indiana since the mid-19th century and used to build and embellish America's most distinguished architectural landmarks, including Washington's National Cathedral, the Empire State Building, Rockefeller Center, the United States Archives, and Grand Central Station. The Land of

Limestone exhibit takes you to the sources of limestone, to the quarries and mills, and commemorates the distinguished legacy of Indiana limestone. The exhibit brings to life the people, events, and history surrounding Lawrence County's famous natural resources, Salem limestone.

Admission: Free.

Directions: Just north of the Courthouse Square Historic District.

FORT WAYNE

Geosciences/Museum

Indiana Purdue University at Ft. Wayne
Fort Wayne, IN 46805
www.ipfw.edu

Open: 7:00 A.M.–10:00 P.M. Closed for all school breaks.

Info: Hallway displays show 285 mineral specimens, 19 meteorite specimens and 92 rock specimens. There is also a Geogarden consisting of a number of large boulder-sized local specimens on display outside in a garden setting.

Admission: Free.

Directions: Call for directions.

INDIANAPOLIS

Museum

Indiana State Museum
650 W. Washington Street
Indianapolis, IN 46204
Phone: (317) 232-1637
Fax: (317) 232-7090
www.indianamuseum.org

Open: All year, 9:00 A.M.–5:00 P.M. Monday–Saturday, 11:00 A.M–6:00 P.M. Sunday. Closed major holidays.

Info: The new Indiana State Museum in White Rock State Park opened on May 22, 2002 and contains exhibits on Indiana's natural history. The building construction included Indiana stones such as limestone and sandstone.

The museum now displays mineral suites which present minerals from Indiana and the surrounding regions. Galleries tell the story of Indiana's natural history, and hands-on activities teach geologic processes.

Admission: Adults $7.00, seniors (above 60) $6.50, children (3–12) $4.00.

Directions: Just west of the corner of West and Washington streets in downtown Indianapolis, in White River State Park. Parking is available in the underground garage off Washington Street.

RICHMOND

Museum

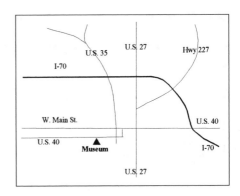

Joseph Moore Museum of Natural
History
Earlham College
Drawer 68
Richmond, IN 47374
Phone: (765) 983-1303
www.earlham.edu/~muse

Open: Monday, Wednesday, and Friday
1:00 – 4:00 P.M. Sunday 1:00 – 5:00 P.M
Info: The museum was established in
1847 as a teaching collection. The geology exhibit displays geological specimens
from the local Ordovician limestone.

As a college program, the museum
hours reflect the academic schedule. The
museum is staffed almost entirely by
students, who design exhibits, maintain
collections, and lead tours.
Admission: Free; donations welcome.
Directions: The museum is located in
Richmond on U.S. 40, west of the river.
From I-70, take the U.S. 35 exit south
until you come to U.S. 40, then turn right.

SECTION 3: Special Events and Tourist Information

TOURIST INFORMATION

State Tourist Agency

Indiana Department of Commerce
Indiana Tourism Division
One North Capitol, Suite 700
Indianapolis, IN 46204-2288
Phone: (317) 233-6886;
(888) ENJOYIN
E-mail: webmaster@enjoyindiana.com
www.enjoyindiana.com

The Story of Maine Tourmaline

A band of mineralization runs from the Maine coast at Brunswick through Auburn and Newry and into New Hampshire. In this area or band are found Maine tourmaline and other gems and minerals. This band of mineralization was formed 300 million years ago when intense volcanic activity resulted in lava flowing into cracks in the existing granite rock. As the lava and surrounding rock cooled, gems and mineral crystals formed in voids in the rock. Over the intervening time, rain and glaciers have eroded the overlying rock, bringing the crystal-bearing voids near or to the surface. In some instances, the rock was so eroded that the crystals were released into the soil and washed down the slope. Thus, the crystals are found in both soil and rock.

Maine tourmaline was first discovered in 1820 by two students who spent much of their leisure time hunting gems in the area around Paris, Maine. Late that year, while exploring Mt. Mica, one of the students found an intense green crystal—a tourmaline—in the soil. When the students returned the next spring, they found more crystals and crystal fragments. Crystals were found in a multitude of colors, including green, red, yellow, and white. Tourmaline

has been mined from Mt. Mica for over 175 years; major finds are still being made. A crystal found in 1978 yielded several cut gems, including a blue-green 256-carat stone.

Other major finds have also been made in this band of mineralization. Tourmaline has been found on Mt. Apatite, in Auburn, since 1839, and tourmaline has been mined there sporadically since 1883. The Plumbago Mining Company was established in 1972 following the discovery of tourmaline on Plumbago Mountain. In the following year and a half, over 1 metric ton of tourmaline, much of it gem quality, was recovered.

One unique type of tourmaline found in Maine is watermelon tourmaline, which has a deep red center and a green outer layer. Another type of tourmaline found in Maine but in few other locations is bicolor tourmaline, in which the crystals have one color at one end and a different color at the other. A few tricolor crystals have even been found. Most of the quarries are closed or private, but some collecting can be done.

(Portions of this text are excerpted from "The History of Maine Tourmaline" with permission from Cross Jewelers, Portland, ME.)

MAINE

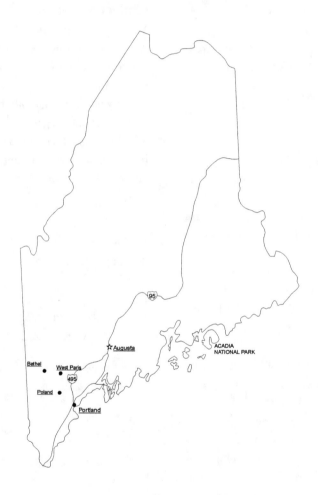

State Mineral: Tourmaline (1971)

ALBANY/ *Native ▪ Difficult*

Collect Minerals in Maine T

The following gems or minerals may be found:

▪ Beryl, almandine garnet, albite, rose quartz, shorl (black tourmaline)

The Bumpus Quarry
Rodney Kimball
Box 6
West Bethel, ME 04217
Phone: (207) 836-3945

Open: Call for days and times.

Info: This is collecting in old gem mine dumps. When the mine was in operation, it produced some of the world's largest beryl crystals. There are still a lot of crystals scattered throughout the mine dumps. You will have to bring any equipment you may need.

Admission: Call for rates. Permission to enter and collect must be obtained from Mr. Kimball, who owns an antique shop on Route 2 in West Bethel.

Directions: The mine is located on Route 5, 7 ¾ miles south of its intersection with Route 2. The mine is located adjacent to the road, at the south end of Songo Pond.

BETHEL / *Native ▪ Moderate to Difficult*

Collect Minerals at a Working Aquamarine Mine T

The following gems or minerals may be found (these have been observed to date):

▪ Beryl (aquamarine variety), quartz (smoky and milky), albite feldspar, black tourmaline, garnet, mica, pyrite, amethyst (rare), zircon, biotite mica, hydroxyl herderite, columbite, rutile, apatite, siderite, urananite, and hyalite opal

Songo Pond Mine
Jan Neal Brownstein
40 Songo Pond Road
P.O. Box 864
Bethel, ME 04217
Phone: (207) 824-3898

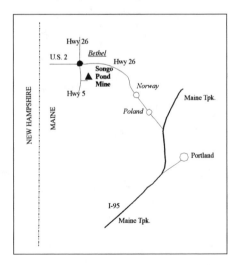

Open: Late spring until snow (November) 8:00 A.M.– 4:00 P.M. Daily admissions are limited. Call ahead—advance reservations required.

July and August, 8:00 A.M.–noon, 7 days/week (more or less). Site may be closed to visitors during certain mining operations or inclement weather.

Info: The mine is open to the public on a seasonal basis and gives a chance to collect minerals from the mine tailings (dump area) and observe a small-scale mining operation at the same time. Bring your own equipment (hammer, chisel, scraper, shovel, screen, etc.). Boots, safety glasses, gloves, and hats are recommended for protective clothing, along with sunscreen. Also, bring something to drink and whatever you will need to eat.

Admission: Adults $10.00, children 7–13 $5.00, children under 6 free. Collection limit: one 5-gallon pail. Groups call ahead for a discount.

Other services available: Shop sells jewelry, gemstones, and mineral specimens. A portable toilet provided at the mine.

Directions: From Route 26 or Route 2, travel to the town of Bethel; you will see a sign for Route 5 south. Travel 4 miles south to the south shore of Songo Pond, then look for a highway sign for South Shore Lane, which is a dirt road on the left. Take South Shore Lane, and the mine parking lot is ¼ mile on the right. The mine sign will indicate if the mine is open or closed; call ahead to ensure that the mine is open.

The parking lot is a 5–10-minute walk from the mine. Handicapped and elderly persons may use limited parking at the top of the hill, 150 feet from the mine. Others may drive up and leave passengers and tools at the mine, then drive back down to the parking lot at the bottom.

POLAND / *Native ▪ Moderate to Difficult*

Camp and Collect Minerals in Maine *T*

The following gems or minerals may be found:

▪ **Tourmaline, beryl, garnet, mica, quartz, albite, columbite, rutile, apatite, and other Maine gems and minerals** (See complete list on page 61)

Poland Mining Camps
Dudy and Mary Groves
P.O. Box 26
Poland, ME 04274
Phone: (207) 998-2350

Open: June 1–October 1 by appointment only.

Info: Collect minerals at pegmatite quarries closed to the public. Poland Mining Camps have exclusive collection access at Mount Mica Quarry, Emmons Quarry, Mount Apatite, Pulsifer Quarry, Keith Quarry, Wade Quarry, Hole-in-the-Ground Quarry, Dionne Quarry, Marie Luise Hopfe Quarry, and others.

This is a unique vacation opportunity. Fee includes lodging, all meals, mine

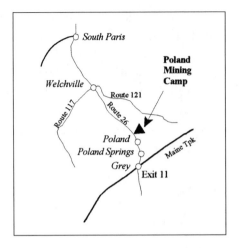

fees, and a guide to famous and active quarries. Lodging is in cabins with two private bedrooms, living room with fireplace (only heat for the cabin), kitchen with fridge, etc., and bath with flush facilities and shower (hot and cold). All linens, bedding, and towels are provided. At the center of the camp complex is a pavilion, which is the hub of activity at the camp. It is used for meals, functions, and general socializing with other campers. Minerals are displayed from the various quarries where you hunt for gems, and lectures and demonstrations by local craftsmen and miners are presented there.

Dudy Groves has over 30 years of experience in mining and collecting gemstones and minerals in the local quarries. He has worked for and/or mined in many of the historically important mining operations, including Mount Apatite and Mount Mica. Mary Groves is in charge of the large organic garden, which supplies much of the food for the camp. She is famous for her down-home cooking and will cater to any special dietary needs.

Fee: $550.00 per person per week for cabins, $100.00 per person per day for a 3-day stay (minimum length of stay). Must provide your own equipment, protective clothing, and transportation. Reservations and a nonrefundable 50% deposit required. Walk-ins will be accommodated only if space is available.

Serious mineral collectors who can't stay at Poland Mining Camps may still join the resident clients on selected days and collect at the Quarry-of-the-Day, selected by Poland Mining Camps. The Tag-a-long Package includes quarry access, quarry fees, up to 7 hours of collecting time (dependent on travel times and other variables), liability coverage, and the services of the guide. It does not include food, lodging, transportation, or other services of the Camps. With the Tag-a-long Package, which requires a reservation, you must join the caravan leaving Poland Mining Camps at 8:00 A.M. and leave the quarry when the guide leaves. Tag-a-long customers must follow all rules and restrictions of Poland Mining Camps and must stay with and follow directions of the Poland Mining Camps guide. You may not enter or return to the Quarry-of-the-Day on your own at any time.

Tag-a-Long Rates: $60.00 per person per day; 10% discount for 3 consecutive days. Prices subject to change.

Minerals List
(Some of the More Common Minerals That May Be Found)

Apatite (fluor-)
Apatite (hydroxyl-)
Albite
Albite (cleavelandite var.)
Almandine garnet
Arsenopyrite
Autenite
Beryl (aquamarine, morganite, goshenite)
Beryllonite
Bertrandite
Biotite mica

Casserite
Columbite
Gahnite (spinel)
Hydroxyl-Herderite
Kaolinite
Lepidolite mica
Lithiophillite
Lollingite
Microcline/orthoclase (feldspar)
Montebrasite
Montmorillonite
Muscovite mica

Petalite
Pollucite
Pyrite
Quartz
Rhodochrosite
Spodumene
Topaz
Tourmaline (elbaite)
Tourmaline (schorl)
Triphyllite
Uranite
Zircon

Phosphate Species Minerals
(That May Be Found in Addition to the Ones Listed Above)

Augelite
Beraumite
Bermanite
Brazilianite
Childrenite
Diadochite
Dickinsonite
Earlshannonite
Eosphorite
Farifieldite
Gainsite
Goyazite
Graftonite
Heterosite

Hureaylite
Jahnsite
Kosnarite
Landsite
Laueite
Ludlamite
McCrillisite
Mitridatite
Monzaite
Moraesite
Perhamite
Phosphosiderite
Phosphouranylite
Purpurite

Reddingite
Rochbridgeite
Stewartite
Strunzite
Switzerite (and metaswitzerite)
Torberite
Triplite
Uralolite
Vivianite
Wardite
Whitlockite
Whitmoreite
Wodginite

Directions: From I-495 take exit 11, Gray. Go north on Route 26 to Poland. Continue north for a couple of miles. Poland Mining Camps is on the right, just before the junction of Route 26 and Route 11.

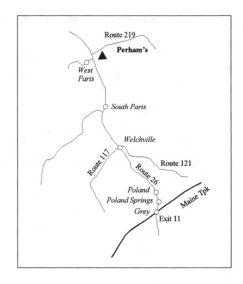

WEST PARIS / *Native* • *Moderate to Difficult*

Collect Minerals in Maine *T*

The following gems or minerals may be found:

▪ Tourmaline (including green and black); beryl; garnet; mica; scheelite; quartz crystals; smoky, rose, and orange quartz; albite; columbite; apatite; amethyst; spodumene; zircon; petalite; cookeite; chrysoberyl; and other Maine gems and minerals

Perham's of West Paris
P.O. Box 280
West Paris, ME 04289
Phone: (207) 674-2341; (800) 371-GEMS or (800) 371-4367
Fax: (207) 674-3692

Open: Shop open all year, 9:00 A.M.– 5:00 P.M., 7 days/week; from January 1–April 1, closed Mondays. Sites may be closed to visitors during occasional mining operations; closed Thanksgiving and Christmas.
Info: Perham's owns five quarries located within 10 miles of the shop. Information on these quarries is found on the next page. Maps are available free at the shop.

Before going to the quarries, you may study the museum displays to learn to recognize minerals that can be found locally. Bring your own equipment and protective clothing. Keep what you find in your collecting venture.
Rates: May visit quarries free of charge.
Other services available: Shop sells fine jewelry, gemstones and mineral specimens, also prospecting tools, books, and gifts. Museum (for further information, see listing in Section 2).
Directions: Take exit 11 on the Maine Turnpike; then Maine Route 26 north to West Paris, and Perham's.
Important Note: During late October and November, hunting season is open. The land owned by Perham's is *not* posted, so it is advisable to wear blaze orange when visiting the quarries during this time.

Perham's Quarries

Local quarries are all open pits, and collecting usually takes place in the surrounding dump areas, or tailings. Actual mining is sporadic, but mineral collecting is an ongoing activity taking place when weather permits. Common-sense safety guidelines offer adequate protection. What you find will depend upon your persistence—and your luck.

Harvard Quarry

This renowned locale was initially developed about 1870 by George "Shavey" Noyes. Harvard University conducted a mining operation here in 1917, and the quarry was mined by Arthur Valley in 1942. Since 1958 this locale, owned by the Perham family, has been explored sporadically by Frank Perham. The Harvard is noted for fine crystals of purple apatite as well as for green tourmaline, black tourmaline, garnet, beryl, quartz, and cookeite. Amethyst, cassiterite, zircon, petalite, columbite, gahnite, spodumene, scheelite, vesuvianite, and lepidolite are also found here.

Tamminen Quarry

Mining here began about 1930, and the quarry has since been explored by several mining firms. Owned by Nestor Tamminen for many years, this site was a valued source of feldspar. Among the minerals found here are amblygonite, pollucite, cleavelandite, montmorillonite, and altered spodumene. This locale is renowned for especially fine pseudocubic quartz crystals.

Waisanen Quarry

Mining here began in 1931 when Matti Waisanen conducted an exploration directed at the recovery of mica. The quarry has since been mined extensively for mica and feldspar, both commercially valuable materials. Frank Perham's 1963 mining endeavor produced superb specimens of hydroxyl-herderite, bertrandite, purple apatite, and superb parallel-growth quartz crystals. Other mineral varieties found here include gem tourmaline, spodumene, triphylite, and columbite.

Nubble Quarry

Various people have mined this quarry since the 1930 era. It is well known for producing exceptionally fine qualities of mica. Early in the 1940s, mining at the Nubble Quarry revealed the finest grade of mica found anywhere in New England. Mining here has also produced specimens of beryllonite, chrysoberyl, green apatite, and gem-quality smoky and rose quartz, as well as excellent garnet crystals.

Whispering Pines Quarry

This quarry was first mined during the 1930 era by Arthur Valley and later by others. Since 1962 it has been mined sporadically. This is the area's only likely source of gem-quality rose quartz. The locale also produces orange and smoky quartz, mica, garnet, beryl, vesuvianite, and fine crystals of black tourmaline. The Whispering Pine Quarry is an excellent place for the novice to study pegmatite mineralization. Its easy accessibility is ideal for small children.

AUGUSTA

Museum

Maine State Museum
83 State House Station
Augusta, ME 04333-0083
Phone: (207) 287-2301
www.state.me.us/museum/

Open: All year; closed major holidays. 9:00 A.M.–5:00 P.M. Monday–Friday, 10:00 A.M.–4:00 P.M. Saturday, 1:00–4:00 P.M. Sunday.

Info: Gem and mineral cases present a display of Maine gemstones, including smoky quartz, milky quartz, rose quartz, amethyst, garnet, beryl, and gold. Various types of the Maine state mineral, tourmaline, are on display. The Peary necklace, which Arctic explorer Robert Peary gave to his wife for a birthday present in 1913, is on display. It is made from gold collected from the Swift River in western Maine, and Maine tourmaline.

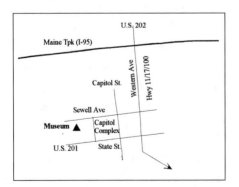

Admission: Free.

Directions: Take State Highways 11/17/100 (Western Avenue) from the Maine Turnpike into Augusta. Turn right onto Sewell Street and drive to the capitol complex.

WEST PARIS

Museum

Perham's of West Paris
Route 26
P.O. Box 280
West Paris, ME 04289
Phone: (207) 674-2341;
(800) 371-GEMS or (800) 371-4367
Fax: (207) 674-3692

Open: Shop open all year, 9:00 A.M.–5:00 P.M. 7 days/week; from January

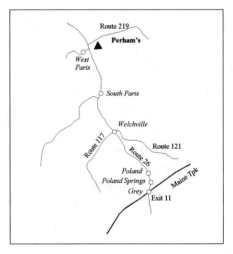

1–April 1, closed Mondays; closed Thanksgiving and Christmas.

Info: Stanley Perham started in the gemstone business in 1919, and the family-owned business has grown since that time. *Museum Attractions Include:*

- Collection of Maine minerals and gems
- Model of a working feldspar quarry
- The MERCROPON gem cutting developed by Stanley Perham and other local men interested in gem cutting, which served as a prototype for the development of modern faceting machines
- A model of a gem tourmaline pocket
- A collection of fluorescent minerals

Admission: Free.

Directions: Take exit 11 on the Maine Turnpike; then Maine Route 26 north to West Paris, and Perham's.

SECTION 3: Special Events and Tourist Information

ANNUAL EVENT

Maine Mineral Symposium, Augusta, Maine

The symposium includes lectures, exhibits, displays, and dealers. Several mineral localities are available for field collecting. Held for 3 days in May.

For registration or more information on the symposium, visit:
www.state.me.us/doc/nrimc/mgs/mincolec/sympnews.htm

TOURIST INFORMATION

State Tourist Agency

Maine Office of Tourism
#59 State House Station
Augusta, ME 04333
Phone: (888) 624-6345
www.visitmaine.com

MARYLAND

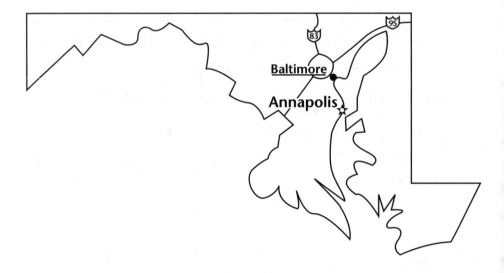

SECTION 1: Fee Dig Sites and Guide Services

No information available.

SECTION 2: Museums and Mine Tours

No information available.

SECTION 3: Special Events and Tourist Information

TOURIST INFORMATION

State Tourist Agency

Maryland Office of Tourism and
Development
217 East Redwood Street, 9th floor
Baltimore, MD 21202
Phone: (800) MDISFUN or
(800) 634-7386
www.mdisfun.org

MASSACHUSETTS

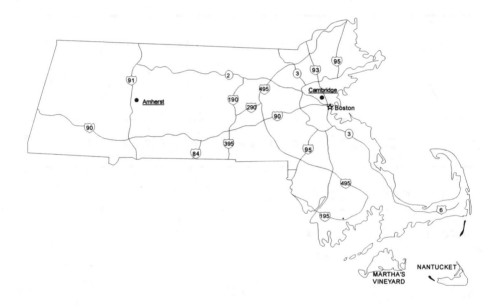

State Gemstone: Rhodonite
State Mineral: Babingtonite
State Stone/Rock: Plymouth Rock; Dighton Rock;
Roxbury Conglomerate

SECTION 1: Fee Dig Sites and Guide Services

No information available.

SECTION 2: Museums and Mine Tours

CAMBRIDGE

Museum 🏛

Harvard Museum of Natural History
Harvard University
26 Oxford Street
Cambridge, MA 02138
Phone: (617) 495-3045
www.hmnh.edu

Open: All year, 9:00 A.M.–5:00 P.M. daily.

Info: The exhibits feature a comprehensive collection of gems, minerals, ores, and meteorites. Begun in 1784, the museum's collections cover virtually the entire scope of the mineral sciences, with 50,000 specimens.

The petrology collection and economic geology collection, comprising suites of igneous, sedimentary, and metamorphic rocks and ores (75,000+ specimens), are an impressive sampling of the Earth's crust.

Meteorites provide insight into the origin of the solar system and the universe. In 1883 the museum augmented its holdings by the acquisition of the J.

Lawrence Smith Collection. The museum has a broadly representative collection of over 514 meteorites.

The museum also has an exhibit on New England gems and minerals.

Admission: Adults $6.50, non-Harvard students with ID and seniors $5.00, children 3–18 $4.00. Group rates available. Free entry Sunday 9:00 A.M.–noon.

Directions: From Memorial Drive in Cambridge, take State Highway 2A (Massachusetts Avenue) west to get to Harvard. At Harvard, turn right on Quincy Avenue, until it ends at Kirkland Street. Turn right on Kirkland and then left on Divinity Avenue. The museum is one block up on Divinity.

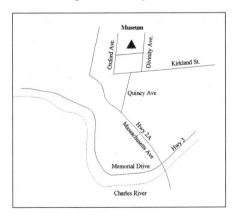

AMHERST

Museum

The Pratt Museum of Natural History
Amherst University
Amherst, MA 01002
Phone: (413) 542-2165
www.amherst.edu/~pratt

Open: Academic year, 9:00 A.M.–3:30 P.M. Monday–Friday, 10:00 A.M.– 4:00 P.M. Saturday, noon–5:00 P.M. Sunday. Summers, 10:00 A.M.– 4:00 P.M. Saturday, noon–5:00 P.M. Sunday.

Info: The collection of minerals at the Pratt Museum contains approximately 10,000 specimens. As you enter the Mineral Hall, you will see a portion of the collection on display in the floor cases. The minerals here are arranged according to a system based on their chemistry. The first case you approach contains examples of the mineral group classified as the native elements: minerals composed of only one chemical compound, for example, native gold, diamond (carbon) and graphite (carbon). As you proceed counterclockwise around the gallery, the mineral chemistry becomes more complex until you reach the last group, the silicates. Models are used to illustrate the complex but symmetrical internal structure of these minerals.

Other wall cases contain exhibits of minerals found in New England. Also included in the mineral collection are meteorites.

Admission: Free.

Directions: On the campus of Amherst College, on the quadrangle.

SPRINGFIELD

Museum

Springfield Science Museum
220 State Street
Springfield, MA 01103
Phone: (413) 263-6800
www.quadrangle.org

Open: All year, noon– 4:00 P.M. Wednesday–Friday, 11:00 A.M.– 4:00 P.M. Saturday–Sunday.

Info: Mineral Hall displays minerals from around the world, including a collection made by two local jewelers. It also has a fluorescent mineral display, specimens of local minerals, and a meteorite from Arizona.

Admission: Adults $7.00, seniors $5.00, college students $4.00, children (6–17) $3.00, children under 6 free.

Directions: The museum is located on the Quadrangle at the corner of State and Chestnut Streets. Free parking is available in the Springfield Library and Museum lot on Edwards Street and on State Street directly across from the library.

SECTION 3: Special Events and Tourist Information

TOURIST INFORMATION

State Tourist Agency

Massachusetts Office of Travel and
Tourism
10 Park Plaza, Suite 4510
Boston, MA 02116
Phone: (617) 973-8500;
(800) 227-MASS or (800) 227-6277
www.mass-vacation.com

MICHIGAN

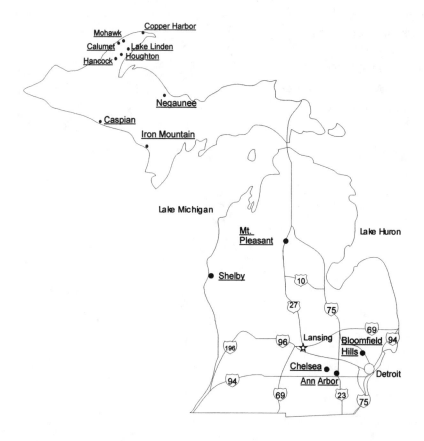

State Gemstone: Isle Royal Greenstone (Chlorostrolite) (1965)
State Stone/Rock: Petosky Stone (1965)

MOHAWK / *Native • Easy*

Find Your Own Copper T

The following gems or minerals may be found:

- **Copper**

Delaware Copper Mine
HCI, Box 102
Mohawk, MI 49950
Phone: (906) 289-4688
www.copperharbor.org

Open: Seven days a week. 10:00 A.M.–6:00 P.M. June, July, August; 10:00 A.M.–5:00 P.M. September–October.

Info: Search for souvenir copper at an authentic copper mine dating back to 1847–1887.

Admission: For further information on the mine tour, see listing under Section 2.

Directions: Located in the historic ghost town of Delaware, 12 miles south of Copper Harbor and 38 miles north of Houghton on U.S. 41.

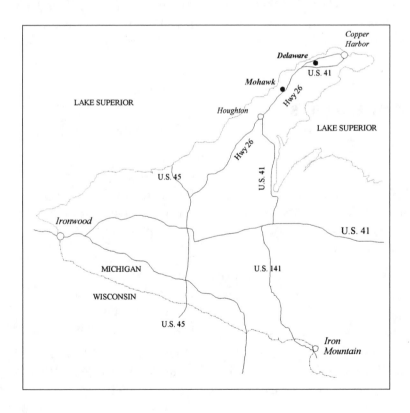

ANN ARBOR

Museum

Exhibit Museum of Natural History
University of Michigan
1109 Geddes Avenue
Ann Arbor, MI 48019-1079
Phone: (734) 764-0478
www.exhibits.lsa.umich.edu

Open: All year, 9:00 A.M.–5:00 P.M. Monday–Saturday, noon–5:00 P.M. Sunday.
Info: The museum has a geology gallery, which displays rocks and minerals.
Admission: Free.
Directions: On Geddes Avenue in Ann Arbor.

BLOOMFIELD HILLS

Museum

Cranbrook Institute of Science
1221 North Woodward Avenue
Bloomfield Hills, MI 48303-0801
Phone: (248) 645-3200
www.cranbrook.edu

Open: All year, 10:00 A.M.–5:00 P.M. Sunday–Thursday, 10:00 A.M.–10:00 P.M. Friday.
Info: Mineral Hall contains numerous cases displaying approximately 5,000 minerals from all over the world. This prize collection of minerals and crystals includes what has been described as an almost perfect hiddenite crystal and what is perhaps the finest gold specimen in the world.
Admission: Adults $7.00, children 2–12 and seniors $5.00, children under 2 free.
Directions: Located at 1221 North Woodward Avenue in Bloomfield Hills. Cranbrook is located on the west side of Woodward Avenue between Long Lake and Lone Pine Roads. From I-75, exit Big Beaver (west) to Woodward Avenue (north). From I-696; exit Woodward Avenue (north). From Telegraph: Long Lake Road (east) to Woodward Avenue (south).

CALUMET

Mining Museum

Summer:
Coppertown, U.S.A.
Red Jacket Road
Calumet, MI 49913
Phone: (906) 337-4354

Off-season:
Coppertown, U.S.A.
1197 Calumet Avenue
Calumet, MI 49913
Phone: (906) 338-7982

Open: All year, 10:00 A.M.–5:00 P.M. Monday–Saturday. Sunday (July–August) 12:30 P.M.– 4:00 P.M.

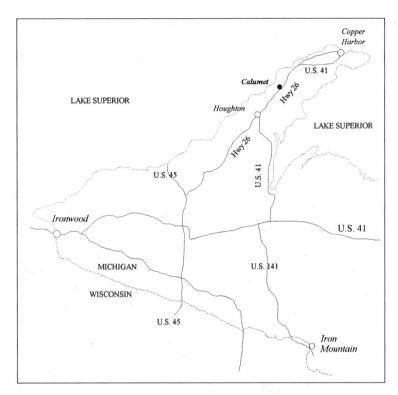

Info: The mining museum is an introduction to the story of the copper country and Keweenaw Peninsula, and America's first real mining boom. Michigan's copper industry began thousands of years ago when ancient miners attacked exposed veins of pure copper with huge hammer-stones. The tools and techniques of mining advanced considerably in the centuries that followed, and Coppertown's mining museum traces this evolution of mines and mining people with a series of exhibits designed for the family visitor.

Admission: Adults $3.00, children 12–18 $1.00, children under 12 free, Golden Age Pass $2.00.

Other services: Gift shop.

Directions: Turn northwest off U.S. 41 (Calumet Avenue) onto Red Jacket Road, and travel 1½ blocks to the museum on the left.

For information on other Native American stone quarries, see listings in Newark, DE: jasper quarries (Vol. 4); Copper Harbor, MI: copper (Vol. 4); Pipestone, MN: pipestone quarries (Vol.1); Hopewell and Brownsville, OH: flint quarries (Vol. 4); and Fritch, TX: flint quarries (Vol. 2).

CASPIAN

Museum

Iron County Museum and Park
Box 272
Caspian, MI 49915
Phone: (906) 265-2617
E-mail: icmuseum@up.net
www.ironcountymuseum.com

Open: May: weekdays 8:30 A.M.–2:00 P.M.; June, July, August: Monday–Saturday 9:00 A.M.–5:00 P.M., Sunday 1:00–5:00 P.M.; September: Monday–Saturday 10:00 A.M.–4:00 P.M., Sunday 1:00 P.M.–4:00 P.M. Off-months and special times by appointment.

Info: Sample over 110 years of history at a park and museum that have been developed at the site of the headframe and enginehouse of the Caspian Mine. This mine was originally opened in 1903, and shipped over 6.6 million tons of iron ore before it was shut down in 1937. Besides the head frame and engine house, the park contains a diamond drill rig (reported to be one of only three existing in the world), a simulated scraper drift, a mine ore rail car, and two mining halls containing artifacts, displays, and models telling the story of iron ore mining in Michigan over the last century.

Admission: Adults $5.00, children $2.50.
Other services available: Gift shop.
Directions: Brady at Museum Road in Caspian, off M-189, or 2 miles off U.S. 2 at Iron River.

CHELSEA

Geology Center

Gerald E. Eddy Discovery Center
Waterloo Recreation Area
16345 McClure Road
Chelsea, MI 48118
Phone: (734) 475-3170

Open: All year, 9:00 A.M.–5:00 P.M. Tuesday–Sunday. Closed state holidays.
Info: The center introduces the world of geology with a focus on Michigan rocks, minerals, crystals, and mining from prehistoric times through the 20th century. Visitors can see displays, exhibits, and a multiprojector slide show. There is also an easy geology walking trail, ¾ mile long.
Admission: A State Park Vehicle pass is required to enter all Michigan State Parks—cost $4.00/day, $20.00/year. No charge to enter the Geology Center.

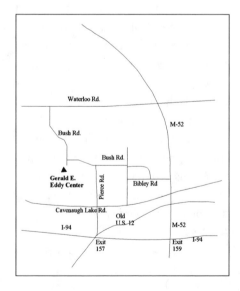

Other services available: Gift shop.

The center is part of the 20,000-acre Waterloo Recreation Area, which features four campgrounds, a swimming beach, picnic sites, and hiking and horse trails.

Directions: From I-94, take exit 157, then take Pierce Road north to Bush Road. When Pierce Road ends, turn left to Bush Road, then left again to the Geology Center.

COPPER HARBOR

Mine tour

Fort Wilkins State Park
P.O. Box 71
Copper Harbor, MI 49918
Phone: (906) 289-4215
www.michigan.gov/dnr

Open: Early-May–early-October, daily 8:00 A.M.–dusk.

Info: The interpretation of copper mining in the Copper Harbor region between 1840 and 1860 takes place in three locations at the State Park. One is within the fort, showing all phases of mining, beginning with the initial discovery and

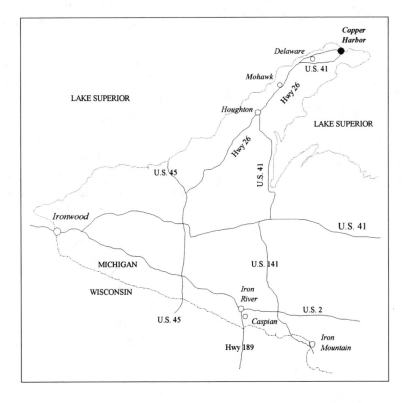

including Native American artifacts. A map shows the underlying geography and location of several old mine shafts. An interpretive walking trail at the lighthouse complex takes the visitor to the still-visible remains of a copper silicate vein (which gave Copper Harbor its name) and to the site of the first commercial copper mine in Michigan. Finally, there are several other mining pits located within the grounds of the fort, some of which have interpretive information.

Admission: A State Park Vehicle pass is required to enter all Michigan State Parks—cost $4.00/day, $20.00/year.

Directions: Take U.S. 45 north from the Michigan-Wisconsin border to State Highway 26. Take Highway 26 north to Copper Harbor.

For information on other Native American stone quarries, see listings in Newark, DE: jasper quarries (Vol. 4); Calumet, MI: copper (Vol. 4); Pipestone, MN: pipestone quarries (Vol.1); Hopewell and Brownsville, OH: flint quarries (Vol. 4); and Fritch, TX: flint quarries (Vol. 2).

HANCOCK

Museum/Mine Tour

The Quincy Mining Company
201 Royce Road
Hancock, MI 49930
Phone: (906) 482-3101
Fax: (906) 482-5569
www.quincymine.com

Open: 9:30 A.M.–5:00 P.M. Monday–Saturday, 11:00 A.M.–5:00 P.M. Sunday; after Labor Day: 10:30 A.M.–4:00 P.M. Monday–Saturday, 12:30–4:00 P.M. Sunday.

Info: First-hand glimpse of what our nation's first mineral boom was like. Visitors will experience a total copper mining experience, including visits to the steam hoist buildings, the Number Two Shafthouse, and the underground copper mine. The Quincy Steam Hoist is the world's largest steam-driven hoist and was first operational in 1920. The underground mine tour includes the East Adit and the experimental mine run by the Michigan Technological University.

Admission: Full mine tour and surface tour, adults $12.50, children $7.00, children under 5 free. Surface mine tour and train ride, adults $7.50, children 6–13 $2.50.

Other services available: Gift shop.

Directions: Located on Route U.S. 41 North in Hancock.

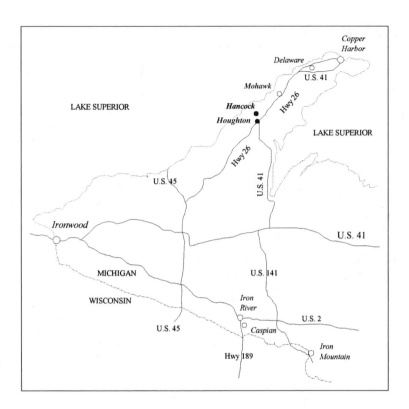

HOUGHTON

Museum 🏛

The A. E. Seaman Mineral Museum
Michigan Technological University
1400 Townsend Drive
Houghton, MI 49931-1295
Phone: (906) 487-2572
Fax: (906) 487-3027

Open: All year, 9:00 A.M.–4:30 P.M. Monday–Friday, noon–4:00 P.M. Saturday (July–October). Closed on university holidays. Group tours by prior arrangement.
Info: The A. E. Seaman Mineral Museum is recognized worldwide for having one of the premier crystal collections in North America. It has the world's finest display of minerals from the Lake Superior Copper District. The museum's collections include an irreplaceable heritage of minerals from the great copper-mining days of Michigan's Keweenaw Peninsula. Also on display are minerals from Europe, China, and Russia.
Admission: Free; donations appreciated.
Other services available: Mineral identification by prior arrangement.
Directions: The museum is located on the fifth floor of the Electrical Energy Resources Center (EERC) on the campus of the Michigan Technological University.

IRON MOUNTAIN

Mine Tour

Iron Mountain Iron Mine
P.O. Box 177
Iron Mountain, MI 49801
Phone: (906) 563-8077
Off-season: (906) 774-7914
E-mail: ironmine@uplogon.com

Open: Memorial Day–October 15, 9:00 A.M.–5:00 P.M. Special arrangements can be made for groups.

Info: This is the largest public tour iron mine. Ride an underground mine train through 2,600 feet of underground drifts and tunnels to a depth of 400 feet below the earth's surface. Watch expert miners operate modern mining equipment. Get a free iron ore sample.

Admission: Adults $7.00, children 6–12 $6.00, children under 6 free.

Other services: Large and well-stocked rock and mineral gift shop, historical equipment display.

Directions: Located on U.S. 2 in Vulcan, 9 miles east of Iron Mountain.

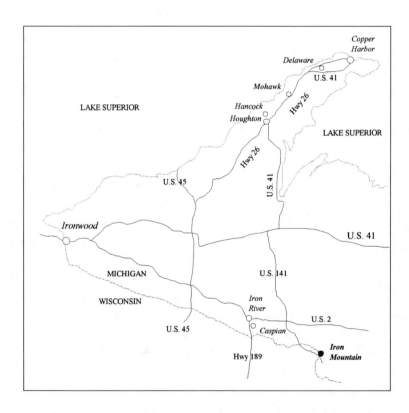

LAKE LINDEN

Museum 🏛

Houghton County Historical Museum
P.O. Box 127
53102 Highway M-26
Lake Linden, MI 49945
Phone: (906) 296-4121
www.habitant.org/houghton

Open: June–September, Monday–Saturday 10:00 A.M.– 4:30 P.M. Special arrangements can be made for groups.

Info: The museum is located in the former main mill office of the Calumet & Hecla Mining Company, built in 1917. Displays include mining equipment and copper refining equipment.

Admission: Adults $5.00, children 12 – 18 and seniors $3.00, children 6–12 $1.00.

Other services available: The Historical Museum Complex includes eight historic buildings, on 15 acres of land, which depict life in the early days in the upper Michigan peninsula's copper country.

Directions: Located on Highway M-26 north from the Portage Lake Lift Bridge or south from Laurium.

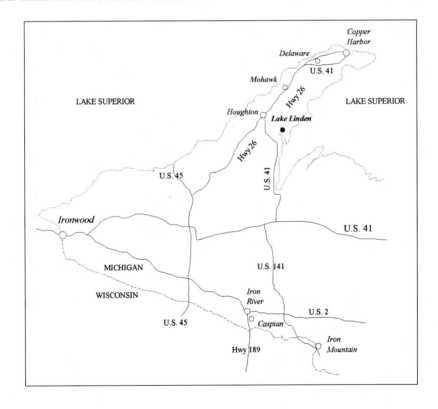

MOHAWK

Mine Tour

Delaware Copper Mine
HCI, Box 102
Mohawk, MI 49950
Phone: (906) 289-4688
www.copperharbor.org

Open: May–October. May, June, September, October 10:00 A.M.–5:00 P.M., last tour at 4:15 P.M. July, August 10:00 A.M.–6:00 P.M., last tour at 5:15 P.M. Special arrangements can be made for groups.

Info: Tour an authentic copper mine that dates back to 1847. Two tours are available. (1) The self-guided tour, where you can take your time and examine the shafts and tunnels, runs from Mid-May through June and from September through mid-October. (2) The guided tour goes down Shaft #1 to the first level at a depth of 110 feet and lasts about 45 minutes, and is followed by an above-ground walk through the mine site. The guided tour is offered in July and August.

Jackets and walking shoes are recommended, as it is 45°F in the mine. Searching for souvenir copper is allowed (no metal detectors).

Admission: Adults 13 and up $8.50, children 6–12 $4.50, children under 6 free.

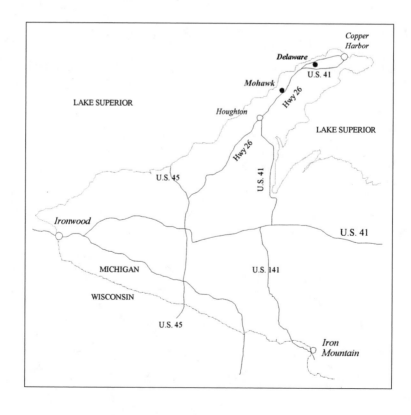

Other services available: Rock and mineral displays, refreshments, copper souvenirs, mini-zoo, mining displays, copper art, walking trails, antique engines, gift shop.

Directions: The mine is located in the historic ghost town of Delaware, which is 12 miles south of Copper Harbor and 38 miles north of Houghton on U.S. 41.

MOUNT PLEASANT

Museum

The Museum of Cultural and Natural History
Central Michigan University
103 Rowe Hall
Mount Pleasant, MI 48859
Phone: (517) 774-3829
www.museum.cmich.edu

Open: Monday–Friday 8:00 A.M.–5:00 P.M., closed noon–1:00 P.M.

Info: The museum has a small collection of rocks and minerals and includes a display of rocks and minerals of Michigan, as well as what is believed to be the largest Petoskey Stone ever found (420 pounds).

Admission: Free.

Directions: The museum is located in Rowe Hall, on Bellows Street just west of Business Route U.S. 27 (Mission Street). Park free in Lot 14 with a permit from the campus Department of Public Safety.

NEGAUNEE

Museum 🏛

Michigan Iron Industry Museum
73 Forge Road
Negaunee, MI 49866-9532
Phone: (906) 475-7857

Open: May 1–October 31, 9:30 A.M.–4:30 P.M. 7 days/week.

Info: Dedicated to the story of Michigan's iron industry, which began in 1848 and continues today, the museum interprets Michigan's three iron ranges and the people who worked them. The museum overlooks the Carp River and the site of the first iron forge in the Lake Superior region. The museum features many exhibits, outdoor interpretive paths, and an 18-minute slide program, "Life on the Michigan Iron Ranges," which is shown in the auditorium. The Michigan Iron Industry Museum is part of the Michigan Historical Museum System.

Admission: Free.

Directions: The museum is located just off U.S. 41, 8 miles west of Marquette.

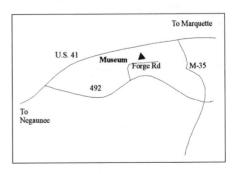

SHELBY

Factory Tour 🏛

Shelby Man-Made Gemstones
1330 Industrial Drive
Shelby, MI 49455
Phone: (213) 841-2165

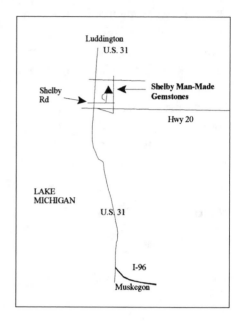

Open: All year, 9:00 A.M.–5:30 P.M. Monday–Friday, noon– 4:00 P.M. Saturday.

Info: Visit a gemstone factory where artificial diamonds are created at an intense heat of 5040°F. Rubies, emeralds, and sapphires in various colors are also made here. Exhibits and shows in a 50-seat theatre present the story of artificial gemstones.

Admission: Free.

Other services available: Gift shop with a complete line of jewelry.

Directions: Shelby Man-Made Gemstones is located on Industrial Drive in Shelby. Take U.S. 31 north from Muskegon to State Highway 20. Exit and get on "old" 31; turn north on old 31 to Shelby Road, then turn west on Shelby Road to Industrial Drive.

SECTION 3: Special Events and Tourist Information

TOURIST INFORMATION

State Tourist Agency

Travel Michigan
P.O. Box 30226
Lansing, MI 48909
Phone: (888) 784-7328
www.michigan.org

NEW HAMPSHIRE

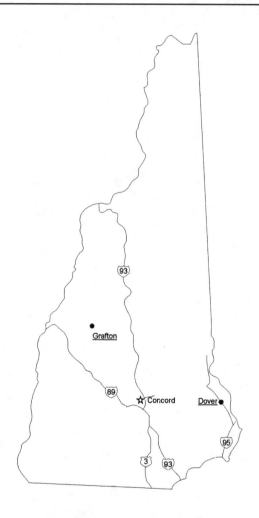

State Gemstone: Smoky Quartz
State Mineral: Beryl
State Stone/Rock: Granite

GRAFTON / *Native • Moderate to Difficult*

Collect up to 150 Different Minerals *T*

The following gems or minerals may be found:

• Mica, topaz, aquamarine, feldspar, beryl, chrysoberyl, amethyst and other quartz minerals, garnet, uranium minerals, tourmaline, columbite, molybdenite, pyrite, purpurite, zircon, and many others

(See complete list below)

Ruggles Mine
Geraldine Searles
Grafton, NH 03240
Phone: (603) 523-4275
www.rugglesmine.com

Some of the Minerals Found at Ruggles Mine

Albite	Feldspar	Quartz (rose, smoky, white)
Amethyst	Fluorapatite	Quartz crystals
Apatite	Garnet	Reddingtite
Autenite	Graftonite	Safflorite
Amphibolite	Gummite	Sillmanite
Aplite	Kasolite	Soddylite (pseudo-uranite, dense yellow)
Aquamarine	Lepidolite (lemon yellow)	Staurolite
Bertranite	Lepidomelane	Tobernite
Beryl (golden, blue, aqua)	Lithiophyllite	Topaz crystals
Biotite	Marcasite	Tourmaline (black)
Bornite	Manganapatite	Triphyllite
Calcite	Montmorillonite	Uranite (species with gummite, world famous)
Chrysoberyl	Molybdenite	Uranium
Clarkite	Muscovite	Uranophane
Clevelandite	Parsonite	Vandendriesscheite
Columbite	Phosphyanylite	Vivianite
Compotite	Psilomelane	Voelerkenite
Cryolite	Purpurite	Zircon crystals
Cymatolite	Pyrite	
Dendrite	Pyrrhotite	

Secret of Ruggles Mine

It all began in 1803, back in the days of the whale oil lamp, when Sam Ruggles not only discovered mica on his land but knew what to do about it. Mica was in keen demand, for use in lamp chimneys and stove windows.

A shrewd hard-working farmer, he set his large family to working it out, and hauled it to Portsmouth by ox team along with his farm products. There it was consigned and shipped to relatives in England to be sold. (Ruggles was too shrewd to sell to American buyers lest they learn the secret of his mine.) Soon, however, the demand for his fine product became so great that special trips to the port were necessary. These were made in the dead of night by horse and buggy, or sleigh, according to season. This continued for several years.

The mine is famous for its huge books of mica, measuring 3–4 feet across and weighing over 100 pounds. General Electric once worked this mine and others in the area for mica. The Bon Ami Company operated the mine from 1932 to 1959 for feldspar, mica, and beryl. Feldspar production during this period ran about 10,000 tons per year. During this time, one mass of beryl was found that filled three freight cars and paid for an entire year's operation.

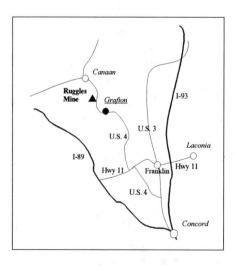

Open: Weekends, mid-May–mid-June; daily mid-June–mid-October; 9:00 A.M.–5:00 P.M., July and August 9:00 A.M.–6:00 P.M. Last ticket sold 1 hour before closing.

Info: Commercial production of mica began in 1803 at the Ruggles Mine. It also is known for the production of beryl and feldspar. Located on the top of Isinglass Mountain, the mine now consists of open pits, giant rooms, and up to 1/3 mile of tunnels with arched ceilings. Its uranium minerals, such as gummite and autunite are prized by collectors and museums all over the world. Bring a camera—a vast panorama of valleys, forest, and surrounding mountains can be seen from the top of the Isinglass Mountain. Unsurpassed fall foliage!

Admission: Adults $16.00/day, children 4–11 $5.00.

Other services available: Snack bar, gift and mineral shop, restrooms.

Note: Knowledge of mineral identification is a plus at this mine.

Directions: Just off U.S. Route 4, at the village green in Grafton.

SECTION 2: **Museums and Mine Tours**

DOVER

Museum

The Woodman Institute
182 Central Avenue
P.O. Box 146
Dover, NH 03821-0146
Phone: (603) 742-1038

Open: Wednesday–Sunday (except holidays) 12:30–4:30 P.M., closed January 1–March 31.

Info: The museum has 1,300 specimens of minerals and rocks on display, including a collection of local rocks in new display cases.

Admission: Adults $3.00, seniors 65+ $2.00, children 14–18 $1.00.

Directions: Take I-95 to Spaulding Turnpike, then take exit 7 to Central Avenue.

SECTION 3: **Special Events and Tourist Information**

TOURIST INFORMATION

State Tourist Agency

New Hampshire Division of Travel & Tourism Development
P.O. Box 1856
Concord, NH 03302-1856

Phone: (603) 271-2666;
(800) FUN.IN.NH or (800) 386-4664
www.visitnh.gov

NEW JERSEY

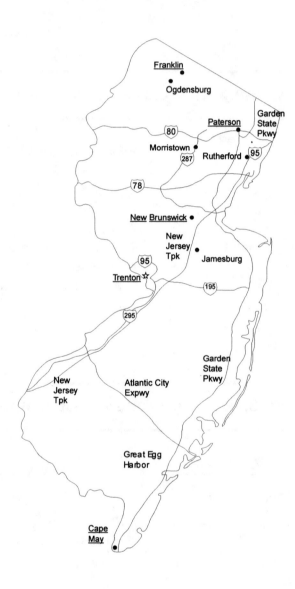

CAPE MAY / *Native*

Hunt for Cape May "Diamonds" on the Beach *T*

The following gems or minerals may be found:

- Cape May "diamonds"

Cape May Welcome Center
County Route 606
Cape May, NJ 08204

Open: All year, dawn–dusk.

Info: Cape May "diamonds" are pure quartz crystals. Their source is the upper reaches of the Delaware River. Some 200 miles upstream from Cape May, pockets and veins of quartz have been eroded. During the thousands of years it takes for these pieces of quartz to make their way down the Delaware to the bay, they are worn smooth. The stones eventually find their way to the mouth of the bay, where strong currents move them along the shores. Eventually some of them wash ashore. The larger stones come ashore mostly in the winter months, particularly during storms, when the currents and waves are stronger. They can be found in abundance on Sunset Beach in historic Cape May Point; currents encounter the concrete ship *Atlantus* here, and the resulting eddies wash the "diamonds" ashore. When polished or cut and faceted, they are said to have the appearance of diamonds. Many people mount them into jewelry items.

Admission: Free.

Other attractions: Dolphin watching, concrete ship *Atlantus*, evening flag ceremony, spectacular sunsets, walking distance to lighthouse and state park.

Directions: Sunset Beach in Cape May.

Cape May "Diamonds" *

The gems are found in limited areas on the beaches along Delaware Bay. They are said to have first been found by the Kechmeche Indians. The Indians attached mystical powers to the stones and believed that these stones possessed supernatural powers, influencing the well-being, success, and good fortunes of the possessor. They often sealed bonds of friendship and goodwill with the gift of these stones.

For other areas where quartz "diamonds" can be found, see entries under Lakeport, CA and Herkimer, Middleville, and St. Johnsville, NY.

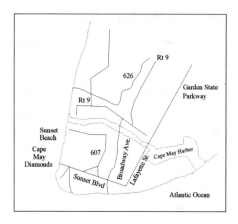

Information and directions may be obtained by calling the Sunset Beach Gift Shops (609) 884-7079.

FRANKLIN / *Native • Easy*

Tailings Digging for Fluorescent Minerals

The following gems or minerals may be found:

- Fluorescent minerals

Franklin Mineral Museum and Buckwheat Dump
P.O. Box 54
Franklin, NJ 07416
Phone: (973) 827-3481
www.franklinmineralmuseum.com

Open: April–November, 10:00 A.M.–4:00 P.M. Monday–Saturday, 11:00 A.M.–4:30 P.M. Sunday, closed Easter and Thanksgiving. Open on March weekends and weekdays for groups by appointment.

Info: Collect rocks and minerals characteristic of the area. Find specimens on the mine waste pile which dates back to the 1870s. Facilities available for testing specimens under ultraviolet light. Abundant specimens are available without the use of tools. A museum exhibit shows what to look for. Ultraviolet mineral lamps and other related items are for sale at the museum gift shop. See the listing in Section 2 for details on the Franklin Mineral Museum.

Admission: Exhibits and Guided Tour (not including rock collecting): Adults $5.00, children $3.00, seniors $4.00. Exhibits and Guided Tour (including rock collecting): Adults $9.00 (for up to 6 lbs. of rocks), children $5.00 (for up to 3 lbs. of rocks), seniors $7.00 (for up to 4 lbs. of rocks). Collecting only: Adults $6.00 (for up to 6 lbs. of rocks), children $3.00 (for up to 3 lbs. of rocks), seniors $4.00 (for up to 4 lbs. of rocks). Additional charge for extra poundage.

Directions: 32 Evans Street off Route 23. Follow blue signs from Route 23 to Evans Street (between Main Street and Buckwheat Road).

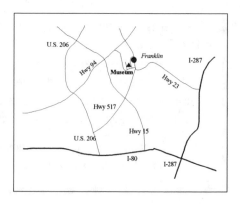

FRANKLIN

Museum

Franklin Mineral Museum
P.O. Box 54
Franklin, NJ 07416
Phone: (973) 827-3481
www.franklinmineralmuseum.com

Open: April–November, 10:00 A.M.– 4:00 P.M. Monday–Saturday, 11:00 A.M.– 4:30 P.M. Sunday. Closed Easter, Thanksgiving. Open weekends in March, and weekdays for groups by appointment.

Info: The museum features minerals, rocks, geology, and replicas of mine workings. The specimens come from local and worldwide sources. The museum features a fluorescent room, where various ores and minerals from the Franklin area are displayed under long-wave and short-wave ultraviolet light. Other displays include gemstones and colorful crystals. The museum's display of over 4,200 specimens is known for its beauty. The new Jensen wing contains the Winifred Welsh natural history collection, a collection assembled by a science teacher for his classes. The displays are impressive as well as educational. The rock collection covers the principal types of rocks.

The Franklin area was the site of iron and zinc mining from 1854 to 1954. Fluorescent minerals from the Franklin area are said to be the world's most brilliant, and specimens from this area are in museum collections across the country. The Franklin area has produced a tenth of all known species of minerals (there are 3,500 known mineral species). All displayed specimens are identified.

Admission: Exhibits and Guided Tour (not including rock collecting): Adults $5.00, children $3.00, seniors $4.00. Exhibits and Guided Tour (including rock collecting): Adults $9.00 (for up to 6 lbs. of rocks), children $5.00 (for up to 3 lbs. of rocks), seniors $7.00 (for up to 4 lbs. of rocks). Collecting only: Adults $6.00 (for up to 6 lbs. of rocks), children $3.00 (for up to 3 lbs. of rocks), seniors $4.00 (for up to 4 lbs. of rocks). Additional charge for extra poundage.

Directions: 32 Evans Street off Route 23. Follow blue signs from Route 23 to Evans Street (between Main Street and Buckwheat Road).

MONROE TOWNSHIP

Museum

Displayworld's Stone Museum
Displayworld, Inc.
608 Spotswood-Englishtown Road
(Route 613)
Monroe Township, NJ 08831
Phone: (732) 521-2232
Fax: (732) 521-3388
E-mail:displayworld@erols.com
www.displayworld.com

Open: April 1–December 23, 7 days/ week. Monday–Saturday 8:00 A.M.–5:00 P.M., Sunday 10:00 A.M.–5:00 P.M. Closed Memorial Day, July 4, Labor Day.

Info: Museum of minerals (and fossils) with a host of indoor and outdoor displays that are "hands-on" so that visitors can actually touch specimens from 80 countries. Recent additions include an exhibit of fluorescent minerals from central New Jersey. Wander through the grounds and enjoy the lake and six stone waterfalls.

The museum is also a showcase of practical masonry. This 5-acre outdoor showroom has hundreds of full-size samples of every type of stone and stone product. Material on display is available for purchase.

The rock and gift shop contains a wide variety of polished gemstones, jewelry, fossils, collectibles, and carved products.

Admission: Free.

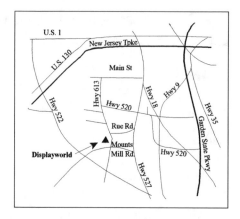

Directions: Garden State Parkway from the north: Take second exit south of Raritan toll plaza (exit 123—Route 9S); follow Route 9 south until you pass under Route 18 overpass, then take first right onto Texas Road (Route 520 West). Follow Route 520 to end, then turn left onto Route 613S; follow 2 miles to Displayworld on right.

From Turnpike exit 8A: Take Route 32 east to Jamesburg (Forsgate Drive), go about 2 miles to end, then right on Route 522E for 2 miles. Pass water tower on left, then drive 2 miles and turn left onto Route 613N. Follow Route 613N 2 miles to Displayworld.

From Turnpike exit 9: Take Route 18S, go about 9 miles to Route 9S. Take first right off Route 9 onto Texas Road (Route 520W), to end. Follow Route 520 to end, then turn left onto Route 613S; follow 2 miles to Displayworld on right.

MORRISTOWN

Museum

The Morris Museum
6 Normandy Heights Road
Morristown, NJ 07960
Phone: (973) 971-3700
www.morrismuseum.org

Open: All year, 10:00 A.M.–5:00 P.M. Tuesday–Saturday (open until 8:00 P.M. Thursday), 1:00–5:00 P.M. Sunday.

Info: The Rock and Mineral Gallery features specimens from five continents, and includes a calcite specimen weighing 258 pounds, and a giant amethyst. Exhibits explore the five geographic areas of the U.S., with emphasis on New Jersey. Another traces the path of a gem from raw material to precious stone. There is also a fluorescent mineral display.

Admission: Adults $6.00, children, students, and senior citizens $4.00.

Directions: At 6 Normandy Heights Road, at the intersection with Columbia Turnpike in Morristown, NJ.

NEW BRUNSWICK

Museum

Rutgers Geology Museum
Geology Building
College Avenue Campus
New Brunswick, NJ 08903
Phone: (732) 932-7243

Open: While school is in session, Monday 1:00–4:00 P.M., Tuesday–Friday 9:00 A.M.–noon. Please call for weekend and summer hours.

Info: Museum features extensive mineral exhibits of specimens from the zinc deposits at Franklin, and zeolite deposits from Paterson. The gallery of meteorites includes a meteorite said to be from Mars.

Admission: Free.

Directions: From the NJ Turnpike, take exit 9 and follow signs for Route 18 North—New Brunswick. Follow Route 18 for about 3 miles. Take the Route 27 South—Princeton exit onto Albany Street. At the third traffic light, turn right onto George Street. Proceed one block on George, pass through the railroad underpass, and proceed through the large iron gates on the corner of George and Somerset Streets. Parking is available in Lot 1.

If traveling from the south, take the Parkway north to exit 105 and follow the signs to Route 18—North, and follow as above.

If traveling from Route 287, take exit 9,

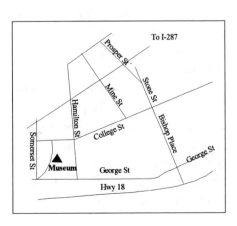

Highland Park River Road. At the fifth light, in about 3 miles, at Metlars Lane, turn right and cross the Raritan River to New Brunswick on Route 18. Take the first exit, George Street. Proceed on George Street to the point where you pass under the railroad underpass, and follow as above.

OGDENSBURG

Museum/Mine Tour

Sterling Hill Mine and Museum
30 Plant Street
Ogdensburg, NJ 07439
Phone: (973) 209-7212

Open: 7 days/week, April 1–November 30, December–March, weather permitting. Giftshop open 10:00 A.M.– 3:00 P.M. Tours daily at 1:00 P.M., other times by chance or appointment. Recommended for ages 6 and up. Group reservations required.

Info: Tour ¼ mile of mine tunnels in the last underground mine to operate in New Jersey. See a spectacular fluorescent mineral display in a natural environment. The museum's exhibit hall contains rare minerals, mining artifacts, and more. The Sterling Hill Mine is a National Historic Site; many original buildings remain, and mining equipment is on display. The mine tunnels are cool, and a light jacket is recommended and proper footwear required for the 1½–2-hour walking tour.

Admission: Adults $9.50, seniors $8.50,

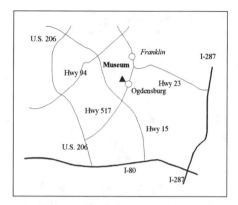

children $7.00.

Other services available: Picnic area, snack bar, modern restrooms.

Directions: From Route 23 in Franklin, take Route 517 south to Ogdensburg. Turn right on Passaic Avenue and drive to the mine. From Route 15 in Sparta, take Route 181 (Sparta/Lake Mohawk exit) to Route 517 north to Ogdensburg, then turn left onto Passaic Avenue, and drive to the mine.

PATERSON

Museum

The Paterson Museum
Thomas Rogers Building
2 Market Street
Paterson, NJ 07501
Phone: (973) 881-3874
Fax: (973) 881-3435
E-mail: patersonmuseum@hotmail.com

Open: 10:00 A.M.– 4:00 P.M. Tuesday–Friday, 12:30 – 4:30 P.M. Saturday–Sunday, closed Mondays and holidays.

Info: There are two major mineralized basalt flows in the world: one in the Deccan plateau of India, and one in Paterson. The minerals found in both locations have much in common, but there are also significant differences. Many of the best and rarest Paterson specimens ever found are exhibited in the museum, along with many fine examples from the Poona region of India.

The museum's mineral collection is one of the finest exhibited collections in the state of New Jersey, with mineral specimens from the state and from around the world.

Admission: Suggested donation: Adults $2.00, children free.

Directions: The museum is located in the Thomas Rogers Locomotive Erecting Building, the focal point of the Great Falls Historic District, in close proximity to the Great Falls of the Passaic River. Paterson is on I-80 in northern New Jersey. Call for directions.

Info: Museum features a collection of fluorescent minerals, about half of which are from the Franklin Mine in New Jersey. The museum also has a display showing the many types of quartz. Another display shows the three types of rock (igneous, sedimentary, and metamorphic), while still another display presents minerals from the Paterson area. The museum also displays about 20 rocks/minerals from Snake Hill (Laurel Hill) in Secaucus, New Jersey.

Admission: Adults $2.00, children $1.00.

Directions: South on Route 17: turn right at Service Road/Local Streets sign, then turn right at Crane Avenue.

North on Route 17: Make jug-handle turn at Highland Cross, then follow directions above.

East on Route 3: Take Ridge Road exit, then turn left on Orient Way at second traffic light. Drive 2 blocks into Rutherford, and turn right on Crane Avenue.

West on Route 3: Take Ridge Road exit, then turn left at the stop sign. Turn

RUTHERFORD

Museum

Meadowland Museum
91 Crane Avenue
P.O. Box 3
Rutherford, NJ 07070
Phone: (201) 935-1175

Open: Monday and Wednesday 1:00–4:00 P.M., Sunday 2:00–4:00 P.M. Call ahead to verify hours.

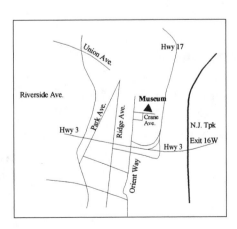

left at the traffic light onto Rutherford Avenue, then turn left at the next light onto Orient Way. Go 3 blocks to Crane Avenue, and turn right.

TRENTON

Museum

New Jersey State Museum
Natural History Office, P.O. Box 530
205 West State Street
Trenton, NJ 08625-0530
Phone: (609) 292-8484

Open: Tuesday–Saturday 9:00 A.M.–4:45 P.M., Sunday 12:00–5:00 P.M.

Closed on state holidays.

Info: The museum's geological collection contains minerals, rocks, sediments, and geological structures. The best mineral specimens are trap rock minerals and fluorescent Franklin/Sterling Hill samples. There is an extensive historic collection of magnetite ore samples from the old iron mines of New Jersey, many of which are closed or no longer exist.

Admission: Free. Parking is free.

Directions: The museum is located in two buildings on West State Street, which is reached by way of the Calhoun Street exit off Route 29.

SECTION 3: Special Events and Tourist Information

TOURIST INFORMATION

State Tourist Agency

New Jersey Division of Travel and Tourism
CN 826
20 West State Street
Trenton, NJ 08625-0826
Phone: (800) JERSEY7 or
(800) 537-7397, ext. 7963
www.visitnj.org

NEW YORK

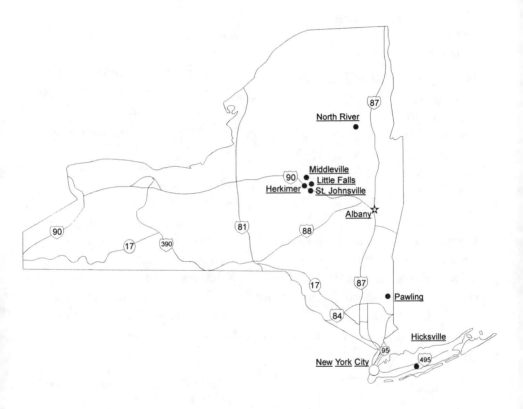

State Gemstone: Garnet (1969)

HERKIMER / *Native* ▪ *Easy to Difficult*

Dig for Herkimer "Diamonds" T

The following gems or minerals may be found:

▪ Herkimer "diamonds"

Herkimer Diamond Mine and KOA Kampground
P.O. Box 510
Herkimer, NY 13350
Phone: (315) 891-7355; (800) 562-0897
Fax: (315) 866-6140
E-mail: diamonds@ntenct.com
www.herkimerdiamond.com

Open: April 1–October 31, weather permitting, 9:00 A.M.–5:00 P.M., 7 days/week.
Info: Herkimer "diamonds" are quartz crystals found in specific locations in New York.

Bring your own tools. Suggested tools include various-sized chisels, a 3-pound hammer, a pry bar, eye protection, and gloves. For the very aggressive digger, a sledgehammer may be useful. Follow safety precautions. The "diamonds" may also be found by simply searching the ground or using a screenbox to sift the soil.
Admission: Adults $7.50, children 5–12 $6.50.
Other services available: Picnic area, playground, mineral museum containing thousands of specimens, gift and mineral shop. Admission free with prospecting, or adults $2.00.

KOA Kampground has sites for RVs with water, sewer, and electrical hookups, tent sites, modern restrooms and showers, ice and firewood, fishing, tubing, swimming, miniature golf, playgrounds, and restaurant. Call for rates.
Directions: From the NY Thruway, use exit 30 and take State Highway 28 north. Herkimer Diamond Mines is 7 miles north of Herkimer.

MIDDLEVILLE / *Native* ▪ *Easy to Difficult*

Prospect for Herkimer "Diamonds" T

The following gems or minerals may be found:

▪ Herkimer "diamonds"

Ace of Diamonds Mine and
Campground
Ted and Anita Smith
P.O. Box 505
Middleville, NY 13406
Phone: (315) 891-3855; (315) 891-3896

Open: April 1–October 31, 9:00 A.M.–
5:00 P.M., 7 days/week.

Info: Bring your own tools or rent tools
at the mine. Suggested tools include a
small shovel, a pick, a garden rake or a
trowel, a 2½-pound pick, and a bucket.
You may want to bring gloves or kneel-
ing pad, and a screenbox.

To stake a claim, place a blue tarp or
tools in your area, not to exceed 10 feet.
You may pay in advance to keep your
claim from day to day.

The mine's conservation rule is as fol-
lows: One pocket only per person or
group. After cleaning out the pocket, the
digger or group must leave the mine for
2 weeks, or a $75.00 trophy fee may be

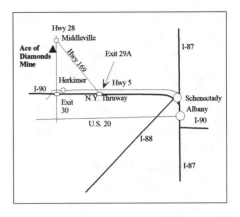

paid by the successful prospector or
group in order to continue mining for a
second pocket. If a second pocket is
obtained, then the person or group must
leave the mine for 2 weeks. The following activities are not allowed at any time:
using sledgehammers over 12 pounds,
using hydraulic jacks in the mining areas,
rolling boulders down the slopes, and
breaking rocks in the camping areas.

Admission: Adults $7.00/day. Take
home all the "diamonds" and specimens

Herkimer "Diamonds"

Herkimer "diamonds" are very brilliant, clear, quartz crystals, which
are double-terminated (points on both ends) and six-sided. They
appear to be faceted by nature, and many are used in jewelry. Rare
ones are found with liquid bubble inclusions. They range in size from
microscopic to several inches. They are found in a rock formation
known as dolomite. The crystals are found mostly in pockets in the
rock; many others, however, are found in the surrounding soil.

Also see listings under Lakeport, CA, for moon tears, or Lake County "diamonds," and Cape May, NJ, for Cape May "diamonds."

you find. Group rates are available (school children with adult supervision $3.00/person, college student and adult groups $5.00/person). To rent tools at the mine, $1.00 each, $2.00 each sledgehammer. Deposit or driver's license is required for tool rental. New tools are offered for sale.

Other services available: Picnic area, snack shop, rock shop, restrooms, camping right where you dig. Within walking distance: luncheonette, grocery store, post office, trout fishing.

Note: All collecting is done at your own risk. The mine is not responsible for injury or loss of personal property.

Campground: $10.00/night for each vehicle and two people, additional people $1.00/night, $3.00/night for electrical hookup, free water hookup, bathrooms with coin-operated showers.

Directions: From the NY Thruway, use exit 30, and take State Highway 28 north. Ace of Diamonds Mines is 9 miles north of Herkimer.

LITTLE FALLS / *Native • Difficult*

Dig for Herkimer "Diamonds" 𝑇

The following gems or minerals may be found:

• Quartz crystals, quartz crystal scepters

Treasure Mountain Diamond Mine
1959 State Route 5S
Little Falls, NY 13365
Phone: (315) 823-7625
www.treasuremt.com

Herkimer "diamonds" can be found simply by walking around the prospecting area or using a screenbox to sift dirt in the prospecting area. The most popular method is breaking them out of the rock. A few rules must be followed:

• Wear eye protection.
• Never break rocks close to someone else. Look in all directions before hammering.
• Keep a close eye on children. Never allow them on top of any high wall or cliff.

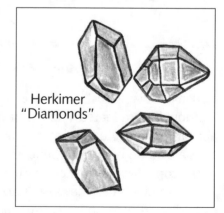

Herkimer "Diamonds"

Open: 8:00 A.M. to dusk.

Info: Digging for Herkimer diamonds can be as simple as just walking in the mine and picking any crystals you may see, or digging in the dirt in the mine. For the more energetic, you can search the loose pieces of rock for crystals, or break the larger pieces looking for vugs. The most difficult mining is to beat on the rock with sledgehammers (no hammers over 20 lbs., please), pry bars, and rock chisels. You will have to bring any equipment you may need.

Admission: Adults $10.00, children 6–12 and seniors over 65 $5.00, no charge for children under 6 and seniors over 80. ½ price after 4:00 P.M. Group discounts available.

Other services available: Gift shop.

Directions: Call or check the website for directions.

NORTH RIVER / *Native • Moderate*

Collect Garnets in a Historic New York Garnet Mine $\int$

The following gems or minerals may be found:

▪ Garnets

The Barton Mine
Bonnie and Peter Barton
P.O. Box 30
North River, NY 12856
Phone: (518) 251-2706
www.garnetminetours.com

Open: June through October, 9:30 A.M.–5:00 P.M. Monday–Saturday, 11:00 A.M.–5:00 P.M. Sunday.

Info: The Barton Mine is called the world's largest garnet mine. The admission fee includes a guided tour of the mine, followed by a demonstration on how to find your own garnets.

Admission: Adults $9.50, children $6.00, seniors $8.00.

Other services available: Mineral shop.

Directions: From Interstate 87, take Exit 23 to Route 9. Follow Route 9 to Route 28, and take Route 28 for approximately 21 miles to North River. At the North River General Store, turn left onto Barton Mine Road. The mine is approximately 5 miles from North River.

ST. JOHNSVILLE / *Native • Easy to Difficult*

Dig for Herkimer "Diamonds" $\int$

The following gems or minerals may be found:

▪ Herkimer "diamonds"

Crystal Grove Diamond Mine and Campground
161 County Highway 114
St. Johnsville, NY 13452
Phone: (518) 568-2914;
(800) KRY-DIAM or (800) 579-3426
Fax: (518) 556-0208
E-mail: fun@crystalgrove.com
www.crystalgrove.com

Open: April 15–October 15, 8:00 A.M.–dusk, 7 days/week.

Info: Use a shovel, hammer and chisel, or small garden tool. If you would rather not break rocks, sifting the dirt through a screenbox will also reveal these gems. Bring your own tools, or some rental tools are available. Suggested tools include various-sized chisels, a 3-pound hammer, a pry bar, eye protection, and gloves. For the very aggressive digger, a sledgehammer may be useful.

Admission: Adults $6.00/day, children under 14 $4.00/day. Group rates available.

Other services available: Picnic area, playground, rock shop with mineral and rock specimens from all over the world. A wooded campground, located at the foothills of the beautiful Adirondacks, is adjacent to the campground. It has water and electrical sites, tent sites, dump station, modern restrooms and showers, ice and firewood, playground, horseshoe pit, volleyball, basketball,

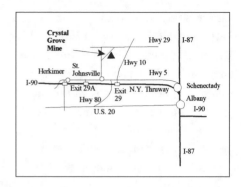

ping-pong. There are many nearby attractions. Rates: $14.00 to $16.00 per day (four people), extra charge for additional persons. Discounts for members of AAA, AARP, etc. RV AC or electric heater $2.00 extra.

Directions: From the NY Thruway, use exit 29 or exit 29A and go to St. Johnsville. Turn at traffic light (Division Street) and travel north ½ mile to a fork in the road. Take the right fork for 4 miles to the campsite. From the north, get on Route 29 to Country Road 114. Take 114 south to the mine.

SECTION 2: Museums and Mine Tours

ALBANY

Museum

New York State Museum
Room 3023
Cultural Education Center
Albany, NY 12230
Phone: (518) 474-5877
www.nysm.nysed.gov

Open: All year, Wednesday–Friday, 9:30 A.M.–5:00 P.M. Closed major holidays.

Info: Exhibits include "Minerals from New York" and a traveling display "Splendor in Stone" which covers photomicrographs. The minerals in the "Minerals from New York" will be rotated periodically.

Admission: Free. Suggested donation of $2.00/person.

Directions: The museum is located in the Cultural Education Center of the Empire State Plaza in Albany, on Madison Avenue across the Plaza from the State Capitol Building. Parking is available at two lots adjacent to the museum; parking there is free after 3:00 P.M.

HICKSVILLE

Museum 🏛

The Hicksville Gregory Museum
Long Island Earth Science Center
Heitz Place
Hicksville, NY 11801
Phone: (516) 822-7505
Fax: (516) 822-3227
E-mail: gregorymuseum@earthlink.net
www.gregorymuseum.org

Open: All year, 9:30 A.M.–4:30 P.M. Tuesday–Friday, 1:00–5:00 P.M. Saturday and Sunday, closed Monday. Groups by appointment.

Info: The mineral collection has approx-

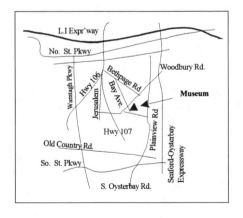

imately 10,000 specimens. Only a small number are on display at any one time. The permanent display features a sampling that serves as an introduction to the major mineral groups. It includes many economically important minerals. Also on display are New Jersey zeolites, Herkimer "diamonds," and fluorescent minerals.

Admission: Adults $5.00, children and seniors $3.00.

Special programs offered include school programs, teacher training, science and craft workshops, and merit badge programs for Girl Scouts and Boy Scouts.

Directions: Located at the Heitz Place Courthouse.

NEW YORK CITY

Museum 🏛

American Museum of Natural History
Central Park West at 79th Street
New York, NY 10024
Phone: (212) 769-5100
Fax: (212) 769-5427
www.amnh.org

Open: All year, 10:00 A.M.–5:45 P.M. daily, closed Thanksgiving, Christmas. Groups by appointment.

Info: The natural history of our planet and its species is revealed in more than 40 exhibit halls. The Morgan Memorial Hall of Gems features the Star of India, the world's largest and most famous blue star sapphire. Among other permanent halls is the Arthur Ross Hall of Meteorites, which features the 4½-billion-year old Ahnighito, the largest meteorite ever retrieved from the earth's surface.

The mineral and gem collection are worldwide in scope. Particular emphasis is placed on exceptional specimens from North America, particularly from the United States. Included are diamonds from Wisconsin and Alabama; rubies, emeralds, and hiddenite from North Carolina; pyrope garnets from Arizona; and opals from the Virgin Valley of Nevada.

Admission: Adults $12.00, students and seniors $9.00, children 2–12 $7.00.

Other services available: Museum shops, restaurants, discovery room for children, theatre, and planetarium.

PAWLING

Museum

Akin Free Library
The Gunnison Natural History Museum
Quaker Hill
Pawling, NY 12564
Phone: (914) 855-5099

Open: May 15–October 15, 2:00–4:00 P.M. Thursday–Sunday. Groups by appointment.

Info: This natural history museum was presented to the community by Olive Mason Gunnison, whose collection covers all phases of natural history. The mineral sections are outstanding, and complete information on each specimen is provided.

Admission: Free.

Other services available: Historical museum, Akin Free Library.

Directions: Pawling is located on State Highway 22, 13 miles north of I-84, near the NY–CT border. The library can be reached by taking Quaker Hill Road 3 miles east from Pawling.

SECTION 3: Special Events and Tourist Information

TOURIST INFORMATION

State Tourist Agency

New York Division of Tourism
30 South Pearl Street
Albany, NY 12245
Phone: (800) CALL NYS or
(800) 225-5697
www.iloveny.state.ny.us

Ohio Flint

Centuries ago, Native Americans from throughout the Midwest forged trails to a range of hills, about 10 miles long, located between the present cities of Newark and Zanesville, Ohio. They came to these hills to obtain flint, and the area came to be known as Flint Ridge. They used the flint to make implements to kill and skin game and to make weapons. The flint in this area occurs in shades of pink, gray, white, yellow, orange, black, and multicolored.

Quarrying for flint was hard work. The flint on the surface exposed to the elements cracked easily; below the surface, a layer of material between 1 and 10 feet deep was of high quality. Large hammerstones weighing up to 25 pounds were used to drive wedges into natural cracks in the flint layer to break large pieces off. Smaller stones were then used to break workable pieces of flint, which were finished as tools or weapons.

Extensive trading networks established by the Hopewell people spread items from Flint Ridge across the eastern half of the country in exchange for such things as copper from the upper Great Lakes and shells from the Gulf of Mexico.

White settlers in the area used the lower grade of weathered flint for making buhrstones for water-powered mills. Smaller pieces were used for hand grinding.

Today, Ohio flint, which is a form of chalcedony, is used by jewelry makers, who polish it and make it into items such as pendants and belt buckles.

For information on other Native American stone quarries, see listings in Newark, DE: jasper quarries (Vol. 4); Calumet and Copper Harbor, MI: copper (Vol. 4); Pipestone, MN: pipestone quarries (Vol.1); and Fritch, TX: flint quarries (Vol. 2).

OHIO

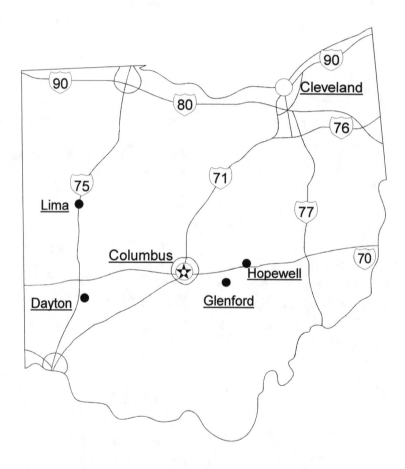

State Gemstone: Flint (1965)

HOPEWELL / *Native • Easy to Difficult*

Dig for Flint $\int$

The following gems or minerals may be found:

▪ Ohio Flint

Hidden Springs Ranch
Gene Wyrick
9305 Hidden Springs Road
Hopewell, OH 43746
Phone: (740) 787-2060
E-mail: gwgenie@alltel.net

Open: By appointment in advance; limited to groups. 8:00 A.M.–6:00 P.M., 7 days/week.

Info: Dig for Ohio flint in a prehistoric Indian flint quarry. Flint occurs in a hard rock environment, so bring appropriate equipment, including safety goggles and gloves. Bring your own bucket! The ranch can accommodate a maximum of 35 people in a group.

Admission: Adults $5.00, children under 12 $3.00, $3.00 per 5 gallon bucket of flint removed, $50.00 nonrefundable deposit required.

Other services available: Hay rides; outdoor barbecues; stocked fishing lake; square dancing; wood for campfires; horseback trail ride; cross-country skiing; campground (primitive campsites for use by tents or campers, $5.00/night).

Directions: Send a stamped self-addressed envelope for specific directions to the ranch.

HOPEWELL / *Native • Easy to Difficult*

Dig for Flint $\int$

The following gems or minerals may be found:

▪ Ohio flint

Nethers Flint
John Nethers
3680 Flint Ridge Road
Hopewell, OH 43746
Phone: (740) 787-2263

Open: All year, weather permitting, daylight hours.

Info: Dig or find your own flint in a wooded ancient quarry area across from the farmhouse. Remember, flint is very

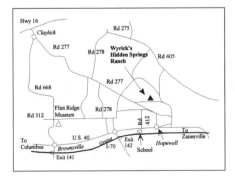

How to Dig for Flint

Today, one can obtain flint in much the same way those Native Americans did centuries ago. The only difference is that today you can use implements made of steel instead of stone.

Because most of the flint is several feet underground, the overlying soil must be removed to expose the flint. There is flint on the surface in some areas, but it is weathered and cracks easily. The normal method used to expose the flint is to dig a pit. (From the numerous ancient pits observable at the various sites, it is obvious that this is what the Native Americans did.) This exposed flint can then be chipped away.

Quarrying for flint is still hard work unless you go the easy route that the authors used and pick through pieces lying in the pits from previous quarrying. The authors collected 65 pounds of flint in varying colors of pink, orange, red, yellow, white, black, and gray. Many pieces contained quartz crystals; even some individual quartz crystals were found. They plan to make cabochons from some of the nice pieces!

Caution: There is a reason why flint was used by Native Americans to make weapons—it can be very sharp. Appropriate caution should be taken, especially if children are involved in the collection. Safety glasses or goggles, gloves, and hard-sided/hard-soled boots should be worn. Care should be taken when working in the "pits" to ensure that the earthen walls do not collapse. *Note:* the authors' daughter, 9 years old at the time, collected flint, did a little quarrying, and even tried to make an arrowhead, without a scratch.

sharp. See the safety notes below.

Admission: $2.00/person for the first 20 pounds, $0.25/pound above 20 pounds. Bring your own tools and protective equipment.

Note: The Nethers allow flint collecting on their farm, but the collecting is at your own risk. No liability is assumed by the owners.

Directions: From I-70, take exit 141 or 142, and drive east on U.S. 40 west. Drive approximately 8 miles to County Line Road (Road 412). Turn left just before the school, and travel north to a stop sign. Continue straight (you will be on Flint Ridge Road) for 1.2 miles. Look for a two-story white house on the right; the flint collecting area is on the left.

CLEVELAND

Museum

The Cleveland Museum of Natural History
Wade Gallery of Gems and Minerals
1 Wade Oval Drive, University Circle
Cleveland, OH 44106-1767
Phone: (216) 231-4600; (800) 317-9155
Fax: (216) 231-5919
www.cmnh.org

Open: Monday–Saturday 10:00 A.M.–5:00 P.M., Sunday noon–5:00 P.M. September–May, open until 10:00 P.M. Wednesday evening.

Info: The Wade Gallery of Gems and Minerals opened May 9, 1998, showcasing more than 1,500 gems, jewels, and treasures. The collection is considered to be one of the top five institutionally owned collections in the United States. The Wade collection includes more than 50 types of gemstones, including colored diamonds, opals, rubies, sapphires, emeralds, pearls, and jade, all of which are now on permanent display. The colored diamonds range from deep, clear green to pale orchid, pink, orange, brown, and blue. The collection also contains one of the largest groups of opals in the country, including black opal from Australia, fire opal from Mexico, and vibrant colored opals from Nevada's Virgin Valley. Jeptha Homer Wade, II, was a Cleveland businessman, philanthropist, and collector of gems and minerals. He was the grandson of the founder of Western Union and was among the first members of the board of directors of the museum. Wade acquired much of his collection with the purpose of donating it to the museum. His granddaughter and grandson have made further donations to his collection.

The jewelry on display ranges from pendants, necklaces, brooches, and bracelets to diamond, gold, and opal rings. Two striking necklaces on display are a rare emerald necklace anecdotally dated to the 1700s, and a topaz and diamond necklace created in 1905 by Tiffany jewelers. The new gallery also presents the spectacular Davidson collection of mineral eggs and cabochons.

Admission: Adults $6.50; children 7–18, seniors 60+, and students $4.50; ages 3–6 $3.50.

Other services available: Museum store.

Directions: Take Euclid or Chester Avenue east from I-90/I-71/I-77.

COLUMBUS

Museum

Orton Geological Museum
Ohio State University
155 South Oval Mall
Columbus, OH 43210
Phone: (614) 292-6896

Open: Monday–Friday 8:00 A.M.–5:00 P.M. Weekend and evening hours by special request.
Info: The museum features geology of Ohio, showing rocks and minerals from the state. Also includes specimens from all over the world. Other exhibits include meteorites (including one that fell in Ohio), minerals, crystals, and fluorescent minerals.

Exhibits illustrate the fundamental concepts about minerals and their physical properties. From the clay tiles in the entrance hall to its wall and foundations, Orton Hall is built of 40 different Ohio building stones.
Admission: Free.
Other services: Free identification of rocks and minerals, museum store.
Directions: Located in Orton Hall on the campus of Ohio State University in Columbus.

DAYTON

Museum

Boonshoft Museum of Discovery
2600 DeWeese Parkway
Dayton, OH 45414
Phone: (937) 275-7431
www.boonshoftmuseum.org

Open: Monday–Friday 9:00 A.M.–5:00 P.M., Saturday 11:00 A.M.–5:00 P.M, Sunday 12:00–5:00 P.M.
Info: Many crystals and minerals are on display in the Bieser Discovery Center, a hands-on area of the museum.
Admission: Adults $7.50, seniors $5.50, children 2–12 $5.00, under 2 free.
Other services available: Zoo, children's play area, space theatre.
Directions: From I-75, take exit 57B (Wagner Ford–Siebenthaler exit). Go west on Wagner Ford Road to North Dixie Drive to Siebenthaler Avenue to Ridge Avenue to DeWeese Parkway. Watch for signs.

GLENFORD

Museum

Flint Ridge State Memorial
7091 Brownsville Road SE
Glenford, OH 43739
Phone: (740) 787-2476; (800) 283-8707

Open: Park open April–October, 9:30 A.M.–dusk. Museum open Memorial

Day–Labor Day, Wednesday–Saturday 9:30 A.M.–5:00 P.M., Sunday and holidays noon–5:00 P.M. Labor Day–October, Saturday 9:30 A.M.–5:00 P.M., Sunday noon–5:00 P.M. School groups by appointment all year.

Info: In 1933, the Ohio Historical Society established the Flint Ridge State Memorial. In 1968, a museum was constructed over one of the original quarry pits (see discussion on Ohio flint at the beginning of this chapter). Exhibits present the geology and history of the site, and the location of other flint deposits in Ohio. In the ancient mining pit, life-sized mannequins show how the material was quarried and then worked to make tools and weapons.

The museum displays a variety of objects made of flint. The shop features flint as a gemstone with locally crafted jewelry. Also sold are books and gifts related to prehistoric Ohio.

A nature preserve with walking trails is located at the memorial. An asphalt path with handrails is available for the handicapped. Also provided are Braille and standard text signs.

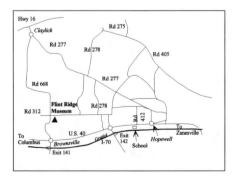

Admission: Adults $3.00, students 6–12 $1.25, children under 6 free.

Directions: Located at the intersection of County Road 312 (Flint Ridge Road) and County Road 668 (Brownsville Road), just north of Brownsville Road.

LIMA

Museum 🏛

Allen County Museum
Allen County Historical Society
620 West Market Street
Lima, OH 45801
Phone: (419) 222-9426
Fax: (419) 222-0649
www.allencountymuseum.org

Open: Tuesday–Sunday 1:00–5:00 P.M., closed Mondays and national holidays.

Info: The museum features an extensive rock and mineral collection, with an entire room solely for the mineral display.

Admission: Free. Suggested donation: $5.00/adult.

Other services available: Library, children's museum.

Directions: Northwest of the intersection of State Highways 309 and 65 in Lima.

SECTION 3: Special Events and Tourist Information

TOURIST INFORMATION

State Tourist Agency

Ohio Office of Travel and Tourism
P.O. Box 1001
Columbus, OH 43216
Phone: (800) BUCKEYE or
(800) 282-5393
www.ohiotourism.com

PENNSYLVANIA

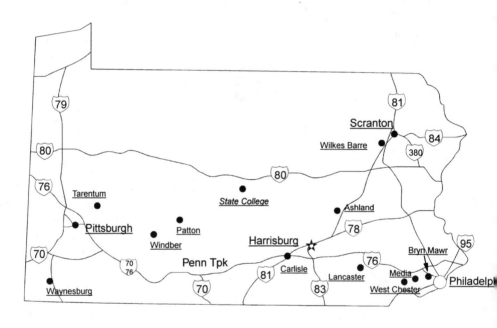

SECTION 1: Fee Dig Sites and Guide Services

No information available.

SECTION 2: Museums and Mine Tours

ASHLAND

Museum

Museum of Anthracite Mining
Ashland Community Enterprise
17th and Pine Streets
Ashland, PA 17921
Phone: (570) 875-4708

Open: May–October, 10:00 A.M.–6:00 P.M. Monday–Sunday. Winter by appointment.
Info: Exhibits and displays present the story of mining and processing anthracite coal.
Admission: Adults $3.50, children 6–17 $2.00, seniors over 60 $3.00.

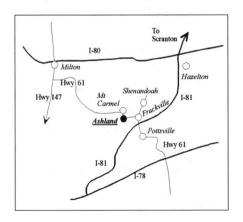

Directions: From I-80, take I-81 to exit 36W (Frackville exit). Take PA Route 61 north to Ashland. From I-78, take PA Route 61 north to Ashland.

ASHLAND

Mine Tour

Pioneer Tunnel Coal Mine
Ashland Community Enterprise
19th and Oak Streets
Ashland, PA 17921
Phone: (570) 875-3850; (570) 875-3301
www.pioneertunnel.com

Open: Daily, Memorial Day–Labor Day 10:00 A.M.–6:00 P.M. Check website for off-season days/times.
Info: Visit an actual coal mine in the heart of Pennsylvania's anthracite region. Pioneer Tunnel is a horizontal drift mine, which runs 1,800 feet straight into the side of Nahanoy Mountain. Ride in open mine cars pulled by a battery-operated mine motor deep inside the mountain. The mine tour temperature averages 50°F throughout the tour, so bring your

sweater or jacket (if necessary, one will be provided to you during the tour).

Admission: Adults $7.00, children under 12 $4.50. Group rates available.

Other services available: Ride an old-fashioned narrow-gauge steam locomotive–powered mine train. See a strip mine, "bootleg" coal hole, and Ashland, a typical early 1900s mining town. Playground and picnic area, gift shop and snack bar. Call for fees.

Directions: From I-80, take I-81 to exit 36W (Frackville exit). Take PA Route 61 north to Ashland. From I-78, take PA Route 61 north to Ashland.

BRYN MAWR

Museum

Department of Geology
Science Center
Bryn Mawr College
Bryn Mawr, PA 19010
Phone: (610) 645-5115 (days);
(610) 388-4148 (evenings)

Open: September 15–December 15, and January 15–May 15 (academic year), 9:00 A.M.–5:00 P.M. Other times of the year by appointment. Group or guided tours available by calling.

Info: View the 1,500 minerals on display in the halls. Approximately 23,500 additional specimens are in the storage rooms.

Admission: Free.

Directions: Bryn Mawr College is located just west of Philadelphia, on U.S. 30.

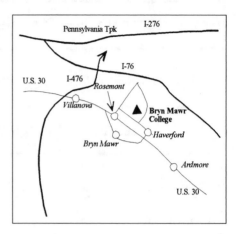

Park in the Science Center lot on New Gulph Road between Roberts Road and Morris Avenue, off Montgomery Avenue near the Bryn Mawr train station. Obtain a parking permit from the department secretary on the second floor.

CARLISLE

Museum

Rennie Geology Museum
Department of Geology
Dickinson College
James Center
Carlisle, PA 17013-2896
Phone: (717) 245-1448
Fax: (717) 245-1971

Open: Monday–Friday, 8:00 A.M.–5:00 P.M.

Info: The museum, located on the first floor of the James Center, contains three cases displaying minerals and one case displaying gems. There is also a fluorescent mineral display.

Admission: Free.

Directions: From Interstate 81, take exit 49 (High Street), bear right at the stop sign, and drive into downtown Carlisle. Go through the square at Hanover Street and continue for a few blocks until you get to College. Turn right onto College, then left onto Louther. The James Center is on the corner of Louther and College. Parking is available on the street in front of the James Center, and the museum is on the first floor.

HARRISBURG

Museum

The State Museum of Pennsylvania
300 North Street
Harrisburg, PA 17120
Phone: (717) 787-4979

Open: 9:00 A.M.–5:00 P.M. Tuesday–Saturday, noon–5:00 P.M. Sunday.

Info: Exhibits and displays explain the basic concepts of geology. Visitors learn about practical applications of geology in displays that present information on materials extracted from rocks, and the everyday products that result.

Admission: Free.

Directions: At the intersection of Third Street and North Street, in Harrisburg, at the capitol complex.

LANCASTER

Museum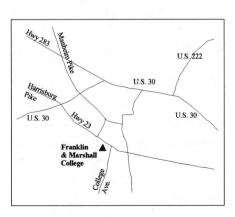

North Museum of Natural History and Science
400 College Avenue
P.O. Box 3003
Lancaster, PA 17603-3393
Phone: (717) 291-3941
www.northmuseum.org

Open: 9:00 A.M.–5:00 P.M. Tuesday–Saturday, 12:00–5:00 P.M. Sunday.

Info: The museum has rocks and minerals on display, with a focus on Lancaster County specimens but also including specimens from around the world.

Admission: Adults $5.50, children 3–12 and seniors over 65 $4.50.

Directions: In Lancaster, on the campus of Franklin and Marshall College, at the corner of College and Buchanan Avenues.

MEDIA

Museum

Delaware County Institute of Science
11 Veterans Square
Media, PA 19063
Phone: (610) 566-5126

Open: Monday, Thursday, and most Saturdays 9:00 A.M.–1:00 P.M., excluding holidays.

Arrangements for group tours can be made by calling the institute.

Info: Display and research collection contains hundreds of minerals from around the world. Many minerals from famous localities in the area are included. The museum houses the original plate blocks used to print Dr. Samuel Gordon's 1922 *Mineralogy of Pennsylvania*. Specimens brought from the mineral prospects of the West by members of the Delaware County Institute of Science during the 1800s can be viewed and studied.

Admission: Free.

Directions: The institute is located in the center of Media near the county courthouse. Media is located west of Philadelphia, near U.S. 1.

PATTON

Mine Tour/Museum

Seldom Seen Mine
P.O. Box 83
Patton, PA 16668
Phone: (800) 237-8590
Off-season: (814) 674-8939
www.seldomseenmine.com

Open: Check website or call for days and times.

Info: Tour an underground bituminous coal mine. Ride an electric mine train into the mine. During the tour, your guide will discuss the past, present, and future of coal mining. Aboveground, view a theatre presentation or tour the museum to learn more about mining.

Admission: Adult $6.00, children 3–12 $3.50.

Directions: Located on Route 36, 41 miles north of Patton.

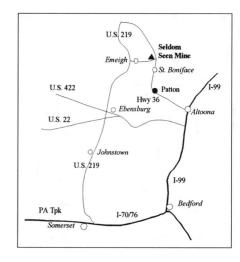

PHILADELPHIA

Museum

Wagner Free Institute of Science
1700 West Montgomery Avenue
Philadelphia, PA 19121
Phone: (215) 763-6529
Fax: (215) 763-1299

Open: Tuesday–Friday, 9:00 A.M.– 4:00
P.M. Arrangements for group tours can
be made by calling ahead.
Info: The institute houses an extensive
collection of more than 100,000 natural
history specimens, including rocks and
minerals.
Admission: Free.
Directions: Take the Broad Street exit
off I-676. Follow Broad Street north to
Norris Street, and turn left at Norris. Go
three blocks to 17th Street, turn left, and
go one block to Montgomery Avenue.

PITTSBURGH

Museum

Carnegie Museum of Natural History
4400 Forbes Avenue
Pittsburgh, PA 15213
Phone: (412) 622-3131
E-mail: cmnhweb@
       carnegiemuseums.org
www.carnegiemuseums.org

Open: Year round; closed major holidays. 10:00 A.M.–5:00 P.M. Tuesday–
Saturday (10:00 A.M.–5:00 P.M. Monday
between July 4 and Labor Day, other-
wise, closed Mondays), 12:00–5:00 P.M.
Sunday. Thursdays open until 9:00 P.M.
Info: The Hillman Hall of Gems and
Minerals, one of the premier mineral halls
in North America, includes specimens
from around the world. Added to the hall
is a case on pseudomorphs, a case on
quartz, and a case on twins. The fluorescent mineral display has been redone. The
collection includes newly acquired minerals from the former Soviet Union. A
highlight of the hall is the collection of
Pennsylvania specimens, including many
from mines that quit producing over 100
years ago. A "float" copper exhibit allows
hands-on investigations.
Admission: Adults $8.00, seniors and
children $5.00, under 3 free.
Directions: The Carnegie Museum is
located inside the city limits of Pittsburgh, on Forbes Avenue in the Oakland
section of the city. From the north or
west, take I-279 to I-376. Take the
Forbes Avenue exit, and stay on Forbes
to the Carnegie Museum and Library
complex. From the east, take I-376 to
the Bates Street exit. Turn right, and stay
on that street until it ends, then turn left.
Take your second right, and follow that
road to the Carnegie Museum and
Library complex.

SCRANTON

Museums, Mine Tour

Anthracite Museum Complex
RR #1, Bald Mountain Road
McDade Park
Scranton, PA 18504
Phone: (570) 963-4804; (570) 963-3208
Fax: (570) 963-4194

Info: Several mining or mining-related attractions are found at or near McDade Park, a reclaimed strip mine in Scranton, Pennsylvania. Some attractions are free; others have admission fees.

Lackawanna Coal Mine Tour: Guided tour 300 feet deep into an anthracite coal mine. See how the "black diamonds" were "harvested" from the earth. Mine temperature is 55°F, so jackets or sweatshirts may be needed. Site also has a gift shop and snack bar. Open April–November, 10:00 A.M.– 4:30 P.M. (800) 238-7245. Admission: Adults $6.00, children 3–12 $4.00, seniors 65 and over $5.75. Located at McDade Park; take Keyser Avenue exit off the Scranton Expressway, travel 3 miles, and turn right at the sign.

Pennsylvania Anthracite Heritage Museum: Explore the history and heritage of the people who settled the anthracite region. Site also has a research library and a store. Open all year Monday–Saturday 9:00 A.M.–5:00 P.M., Sunday noon–5:00 P.M. (570) 963-4804. Admission: Adults $4.00, children 6–17 $2.00, seniors over 60 $3.50. Located at McDade Park; take Keyser Avenue exit off the Scranton Expressway, travel 3 miles, and turn right at the sign.

Scranton Iron Furnaces: Four stone blast furnace stacks symbolize Scranton's industrial heritage. At one time these furnaces were the second largest producers of iron in the nation, and they produced one sixth of the nation's rail output. Tours and events are offered. Open all year during daylight hours; visitors center open 9:00 A.M.– 4:00 P.M. (717) 963-3208. Free. Take exit 53 off I-81, Central Scranton Expressway, to site.

Everhart Museum: Northwestern Pennsylvania's leading museum of natural history. The museum has a variety of exhibits and educational programs on minerals. Open all year daily, 10:00 A.M.–5:00 P.M. (717) 346-7186. Located in Nay Aug Park. Take exit 53 (Central Scranton) off I-81 and follow signs to Jefferson Avenue. Turn right onto Mulberry Street, and go straight to Nay Aug Park.

Other related sites:
- Museum of Anthracite Mining: Located in Ashland; see listing for Ashland.
- Eckley Mining Village: Located in Hazelton; commemorates the history and heritage of the anthracite coal miners.

TARENTUM

Mine Tour/Museum

Tour-Ed Mine
RD2
Tarentum, PA 15084
Phone: (724) 224-4720

Open: Memorial Day–Labor Day, Wednesday–Monday 1:00–4:00 P.M. Last tour at 3:30 P.M. Labor Day–mid-October, open weekends only.

Info: Take an underground tour of a bituminous coal mine. Begin the tour by learning of past and present safety equipment, then board a mantrip car for your journey into the mine. Leave the car and follow your guide to learn about mining methods and machines. After the demonstrations, reboard the car, and return outside. Outside, view displays of surface mining equipment, see a working sawmill, and view a restored 1780s log cabin. The museum contains thousands of items showing what life was like in an early 1900s mining community.

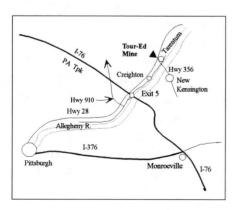

Admission: Adults $7.00, children 12 and under $3.00.

Other services available: Gift shop.

Directions: Located at exit 14 (Tarentum) on Route 28 north from Pittsburgh; 25 minutes from downtown Pittsburgh. From the PA Turnpike, take State Highway 910 to State Highway 28.

UNIVERSITY PARK

Museum

College of Earth & Mineral Sciences
The Pennsylvania State University
112 Steidle Building, Pollock Road
University Park, PA 16802
Phone: (814) 865-6427

Open: All year, weekdays, 9:30 A.M.–5:00 P.M., closed major university holidays.

Info: The main gallery of the Earth & Mineral Science Museum includes displays of fine minerals such as azurite and "velvet" malachite from Bisbee, Arizona, and microcline crystals from Pike's Peak, Colorado. The collection of rocks, minerals, and fossils totals more than 22,000

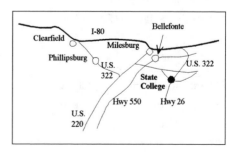

specimens, many of which are on display.

The museum houses the world's most extensive collection of "push-button" electromechanical exhibits demonstrating dozens of the electrical, optical, and physical properties of minerals and materials such as fluorescence, radioactivity, magnetism, conductivity, flexibility, triboluminescence, piezoelectricity, double refraction, resistivity, and much more.

Also on display is an extensive collection of paintings and sculptures depicting mining and related industries, and a collection of more than 100 mine safety lamps and scientific instruments.

A Pennsylvania State Mineral Symposium is sponsored each year.

Admission: Free.

Directions: The museum is in the Steidle Building on the main campus in State College.

WAYNESBURG

Museum

The Paul R. Stewart Museum
Waynesburg College
51 College Street
Waynesburg, PA 15370-9987
Phone: (724) 852-3214
www.waynesburg.edu/visit/museum

Open: Monday–Friday 9:00–noon during the school year. Special tours and summer hours by appointment.

Info: The museum has an outstanding mineral collection, with specimens from around the world. The museum was started in the 1920s by Prof. A. J. Waychoff, who would send back specimens from his travels. In addition, Prof. Waychoff collected many others locally. Other specimens were obtained as donations from alumni stationed all over the world during World War I and World War II.

Paul P. Stewart, Waychoff's nephew, continued the collection when he served as president of the college for 42 years. Some specimens are from a geology field station Stewart set up in Colorado. His will named James "Fuzzy" Randolph, who had been helping with the museum, as curator. Prof. Randolph is always willing to share the many interesting facts and stories behind the collection of the Paul R. Stewart Museum.

The museum is one of the showcases of the Waynesburg College Campus today and could boast of having one of the finest college collections of geological specimens and Indian artifacts in the country. The collections are available for scholarly study.

Admission: Free.

Directions: Waynesburg is located on I-79, just north of the Pennsylvania–West Virginia border. Take exit 3 off I-79, and turn right onto State Highway 21 at the end of the ramp. Follow Highway 21 to the third traffic light, and turn right. Follow this road into town. At the fifth traffic light after the turn, turn right again (at the courthouse) onto Washington Street.

Go two blocks to Miller Hall, which is the large red brick building on the left in the third block. Turn left into College Street in front of Miller Hall, go to the end of the block, and turn right onto Morris Street, then turn right into the parking lot. The museum is in Miller Hall.

WEST CHESTER

Museum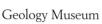

Geology Museum
West Chester University
Department of Geology and Astronomy
West Chester, PA 19383-2150
Phone: (610) 436-2727

Open: During school sessions.
Info: The museum has collections from several noted collectors. One collection focuses on specimens from Chester County, and another highlights fluorescent minerals.
Admission: Free.
Directions: On the campus of West Chester University, in the Schmucker Science Center II.

WILKES-BARRE

Museum 🏛

Wyoming Historical & Geological Society Museum
69 South Franklin Street
Wilkes-Barre, PA 18701
Phone: (570) 823-6244

Open: Noon– 4:00 P.M. Tuesday–Friday, 10:00 A.M.– 4:00 P.M. Saturday.
Info: The museum has a display on anthracite coal mining, which includes a timbered coal mine gangway and its mine railway car.
Admission: Free; donations appreciated.
Other services available: Gift shop.
Directions: On South Franklin Street in the city of Wilkes-Barre.

WINDBER

Museum 🏛

Windber Coal Heritage Center
501 15th Street
P.O. Box 115
Windber, PA 15963-0115
Phone: (814) 467-6680

Open: May 1–October 31, 10:00 A.M.–5:00 P.M. daily.
Info: Housed in an old coal company headquarters building, the Center uses exhibits, media presentations and archives to describe the everyday life of the coal miner and his family, the evolution of mining techniques, unionization, and the impact of the coal industry on small mining towns such as Windber.
Admission: Call for rates.
Directions: The Center is located at the corner of 15th Street and Graham Avenue (Route 160) in Windber, next to the Miner's Park.

ANNUAL EVENT

The Carnegie Museum of Natural History Gem and Mineral Show, Pittsburgh, PA

A 4-day event held the weekend before Thanksgiving, sponsored by the Carnegie Museum of Natural History. The show features select dealers and exhibits set among the exhibit halls and galleries of the museum. Children's activities are also a highlight.

For more information:
Carnegie Museum of Natural History
4400 Forbes Avenue
Pittsburgh, PA 15213
Phone: (412) 622-3131
Fax: (412) 622-8837
www.carnegiemuseum.org

ANNUAL EVENT

Mineralogy Symposium, University Park, PA

This symposium, normally scheduled for 3 days in May, discusses various topics on gems and minerals. A collection field trip is part of the activities.

For more information:
Mineral Symposium
c/o Penn State Mineral Museum
112 Steidle Building
University Park, PA 16802
Attn: Andrew Sicree, Curator
Earth and Sciences Museum
Phone: (814) 865-6427
E-mail: sicree@geosc.psu.edu

TOURIST INFORMATION

State Tourist Agency

Pennsylvania Tourism, Film and Economic Development Marketing Offices
400 North Street
4th Floor
Harrisburg, PA 17120
Phone: (717) 787-5453; (800) VISITPA or (800) 847-4872, ext. 109
Fax: (717) 787-0687
www.state.pa.us

RHODE ISLAND

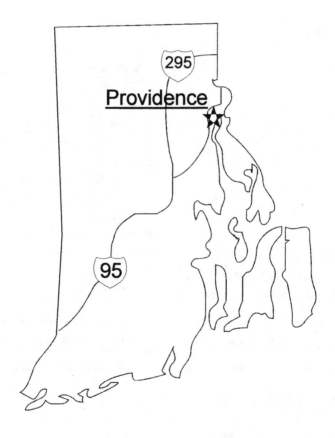

State Mineral: Bowenite
State Stone/Rock: Cumberlandite

SECTION 1: Fee Dig Sites and Guide Services

No information available.

SECTION 2: Museums and Mine Tours

PROVIDENCE

Museum 🏛

Museum of Natural History and
Planetarium
Roger Williams Park
Providence, RI 02905
Phone: (401) 785-9450
Fax: (401) 461-5146
E-mail: museum@osfn.org
www.osfn.org/museum

Open: 10:00 A.M.–5:00 P.M. daily.
Info: Rhode Island's only natural history museum has collections of minerals, rocks, and fossils, assembled primarily by local collectors from around the world.
Admission: Adults $2.00, children under 8 $1.00.
Directions: From I-95 south, take exit 17, turn left at light, then turn left into Roger Williams Park and follow signs to the museum.

From I-95 North, take exit 16, bear right, then turn left at the light onto Elmwood Avenue. Turn right into Roger Williams Park, and follow signs to the museum.

SECTION 3: Special Events and Tourist Information

TOURIST INFORMATION

State Tourist Agency

Rhode Island Tourism Division
One West Exchange Street
Providence, RI 02903
Phone: (401) 222-2601;
(800) 556-2484

Fax: (401) 273-8270
E-mail: visitrhodeisland@riedc.com
www.visitrhodeisland.com

VERMONT

No information available.

BARRE

Quarry Tour

Rock of Ages Corporation
P.O. Box 482
Barre, VT 05641-0482
Visitors' Center Phone: (802) 476-3119
Quarry Div. Phone: (802) 476-3121
Fax: (802) 476-3110
www.rockofages.com

Open: Visitors' center open May 1–October 31, 8:30 A.M.–5:00 P.M. Monday–Saturday, noon–5:00 P.M. Sunday. Closed July 4. 8:30 A.M.–5:00 P.M. Sunday mid-September–mid-October.

Manufacturing facility tour open almost all year, Monday–Friday, 8:00 A.M.–3:30 P.M.

Upper E. L. Smith Quarry tour June–mid-October, 9:15 A.M.–3:00 P.M. Monday–Friday.

Info: Watch granite being quarried, and view finished products being made. Watch videos on granite quarrying at the visitors center, or tour an inactive quarry and collect granite samples for free. For a charge, take a narrated tour of the deepest granite quarry in the world. The visi-tors' center also displays mineral exhibits and geological information, and has a gift shop. There is also a small picnic area and a shop selling sandwiches and Vermont products, including maple syrup.

Manufacturing facility tour: Admission free.

Upper E. L. Smith tour charges: Adults $4.00, seniors $3.50, children 6–12 $1.50, children under 6 free.

Directions: Take Highway 63 (Exit 6) from I-89. Cross Highway 14 and continue up Middle Hill Road. Follow signs to the visitors center.

NORWICH

Museum

Montshire Museum of Science
One Montshire Road
Norwich, VT 05055
Phone: (802) 649-2200
Fax: (802) 649-3637
E-mail: montshire@montshire.net
www.montshire.net

Open: All year, daily 10:00 A.M.–5:00 P.M.

Info: The museum has a limited display of fluorescent minerals.

Admission: Adults $6.50, children 3–17 $5.50, children under 3 free.

Directions: Norwich is located at exit 13 on I-91, just north of White River Junction.

PROCTOR

Mine Tour

Vermont Marble Museum
52 Main Street
P.O. Box 607
Proctor, VT 05767
Phone: (800) 427-1396; (802) 459-2948
www.vermont-marble.com

Open: Mid-May–Mid-November. Call for times.

Info: A theater presents "The Legacy of Vermont Marble," a film showing how marble was formed over 400 million years ago. See the step-by-step process of marble quarrying. Watch a sculptor working.

Tour the Gallery of Presidents: life-sized white marble bas-relief busts of each of the past presidents. Tour the open-air marble market. View the exhibit "Earth Alive" and experience earth's geological history and its ongoing evolution.

Admission: Call for prices.

Directions: Take exit 6 from U.S. 4 in West Rutland. Turn east on Business Route 4 and then north on Vermont Route 3 to Proctor. Turn left over the marble bridge and bear right to the exhibit.

From the north, bear right on Vermont Route 3 from U.S. 7 in Pittsford to Proctor.

SECTION 3: Special Events and Tourist Information

TOURIST INFORMATION

State Tourist Agency

Vermont Department of Tourism and Marketing
6 Baldwin Street, Drawer 33
Montpelier, VT 05633-1301
Phone: (800) VERMONT
E-mail: vttravel@dca.state.vt.us
www.travel-vermont.com

WISCONSIN

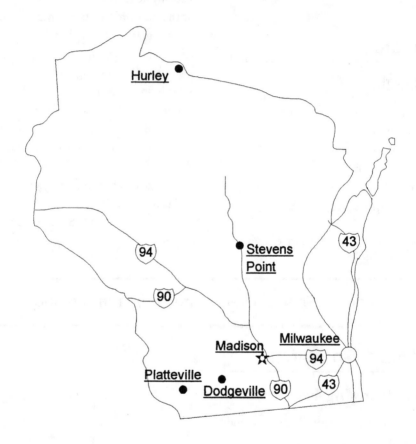

State Gemstone: Galena (1971)
State Stone/Rock: Red Granite (1971)

SECTION 1: Fee Dig Sites and Guide Services

No information available.

SECTION 2: Museums and Mine Tours

DODGEVILLE

Museum

The Museum of Minerals and Crystals
Route 1
Dodgeville, WI 53533
Phone: (608) 935-5205
www.dodgeville.com/members/
Museum_of_Minerals_Crystals.html

Open: April 1–May 15, 9:00 A.M.– 4:00 P.M. September 1–November 15, 9:00 A.M.– 4:00 P.M. 7 days/week.

Info: The museum contains thousands of geological specimens from around the world. Highlights of the collection include a 215-pound amethyst-filled geode, a 315-pound Brazilian agate, and a single 90-pound quartz crystal from Arkansas. The museum also has local specimens and a black light exhibit of fluorescent minerals.

Admission: Adults $4.00, students $3.00.

Other services: Gift shop.

Directions: Located on State Highway 23, 4 miles north of Dodgeville, across from the entrance to Governor Dodge State Park, 5 miles south of House on the Rock.

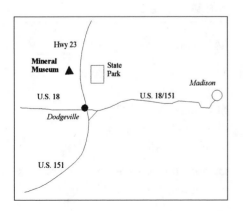

HURLEY

Museum/Mine Exhibit

Iron County Historical Museum
303 Iron Street
Hurley, WI 54534
Phone: (715) 561-2244
www.ironcountymuseum.org

Open: Monday, Wednesday, Friday, and Saturday 10:00 A.M.–2:00 P.M.

Info: This museum has exhibits on the area's mining history. Displays include iron ore and other local mineral samples.

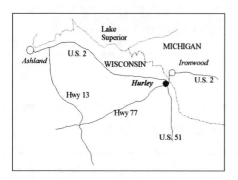

Admission: Free. Group tours, $25.00.
Directions: At the corner of Iron Street and 3rd Avenue in Hurley.

For a nearby related display, visit:
Plummer Mine Interpretive Park
State Highway 77
Pence, WI

Located on State Highway 77 southwest from Hurley. This is the last remaining mine head frame in Wisconsin and is surrounded by an interpretive park that honors the area's miners.

MADISON

Museum 🏛

Geology Museum
Weeks Hall
University of Wisconsin–Madison
1215 West Dayton Street
Madison, WI 53706
Phone: (608) 262-2399
Fax: (608) 262-0693
www.geology.wisc.edu/~museum

Open: All year except major holidays,

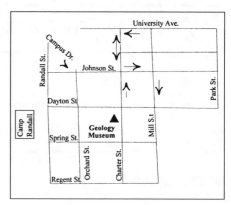

Monday–Friday 8:30 A.M.–4:30 P.M., Saturday 9:00 A.M.–12:00 P.M.
Info: This museum has a mineral collection, which includes a display of fluorescent minerals, and a walk-through model of a Wisconsin cave.
Admission: Free.
Directions: In Weeks Hall on the college campus, at the corner of Charter and Dayton Streets. Note that on-street parking is extremely limited; however, most university parking lots in the vicinity are available on non-football Saturdays.

MILWAUKEE

Museum 🏛

Milwaukee Public Museum
800 West Wells Street
Milwaukee, WI 53233
Phone: (414) 278-2702
www.mpm.edu

Open: All year except major holidays, 9:00 A.M.–5:00 P.M. 7 days/week.

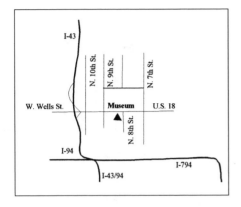

Info: The museum displays some of its over half a million geological specimens from around the world.

Admission: Adults $6.75, children $4.50, seniors $5.50.

Other services available: Gift shop, theater, restaurant.

Directions: In downtown Milwaukee, take the West Wells Street/U.S. 18 exit off I-43, and drive 1½ blocks east. The museum is on the left.

PLATTEVILLE

Museum/Mine Tour

The Mining Museum
The 1845 Bevans Lead Mine
City of Platteville, Museum Department
405 E. Main, P.O. Box 780
Platteville, WI 53818-0780
Phone: (608) 348-3301
www.platteville.com

Open: May–October 9:00 A.M.–5:00 P.M., 7 days/week. Closed major holidays.

Group tours year around by appointment.

Info: The mining museum traces the development of lead and zinc mining in the upper Mississippi valley through models, dioramas, artifacts, and photographs. A guided tour includes a walk down into the Bevans Lead, an 1845 lead mine, which produced over 2 million pounds of lead ore in one year. It also includes a visit to a mine head frame where you can see how zinc ore was hoisted from a mine and hand sorted. A train ride around the museum grounds in ore cars pulled by a 1931 mine locomotive is also available.

The tour of the museum, the mine, and the train ride, along with a second museum tour (Rollo Jamison Museum displaying turn-of-the-century items), take approximately 1½ hours. Comfortable shoes and a light jacket are suggested. Rides on the mine train are included if weather permits.

Admission: Adults $6.00, children 5–15 $2.50, seniors 65+ $5.00.

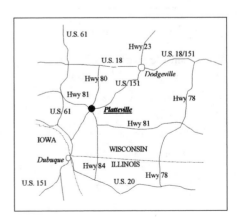

Directions: Platteville is located at the intersection of Highway 80 and U.S. 151.

STEVENS POINT

Museum

Museum of Natural History
University of Wisconsin–Stevens Point
900 Reserve Road
Stevens Point, WI 54481
Phone: (715) 346-2858

Open: During regular semester hours: Sunday 1:00–4:00 P.M., Monday 9:00 A.M.–7:00 P.M., Tuesday–Friday 9:00 A.M.– 4:00 P.M., Saturday 10:00 A.M.–3:00 P.M. Summer: Monday–Thursday 9:00 A.M.– 4:00 P.M., Friday 9:00 A.M.–noon.

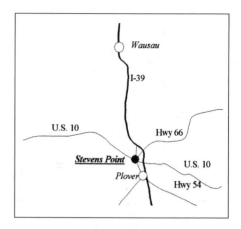

Info: 150 rocks and minerals are on display. Displays show how minerals form and evolve.

Admission: Free; donations appreciated.

Directions: Located on the University of Wisconsin–Stevens Point campus, at the intersection of Reserve Road and Portage Street.

SECTION 3: Special Events and Tourist Information

TOURIST INFORMATION

State Tourist Agency

Wisconsin Department of Tourism
201 W. Washington Avenue
Madison, WI 53707-7976
Phone: (800) 432-TRIP or
(800) 432-8747
www.travelwisconsin.com

Chamber of Commerce

Hurley Area Chamber of Commerce
316 Silver Street
Hurley, WI 54534
Phone: (715) 561-4334
www.hurleywi.com

Information on Hurley's historic mining area, one of the most famous mining towns of all time.

Index by State

ALABAMA

Fee Dig Mines and Guide Services
　　　　None

Museums and Mine Tours
Anniston　　Anniston Museum of Natural History—gemstones, meteorite, artificial indoor cave

ALASKA

Fee Dig Mines and Guide Services
Fairbanks　　El Dorado Gold Mine—gold panning
　　　　Gold Dredge No. 8—gold panning
　　　　Chena Hot Springs Resort—gold panning

Museums and Mine Tours
Anchorage　　Stewart's Photo Shop—gem and mineral displays
Fairbanks　　El Dorado Gold Mine—working gold mine tour
　　　　Gold Dredge No. 8—gold dredge tour
　　　　University of Alaska Museum—minerals and gems from Alaska, Arctic Canada, and the Pacific Rim; includes gold and meteorites

ARIZONA

Fee Dig Mines and Guide Services
Apache Junction　　Apache Trails Tours—gold panning
Goldfield　　Goldfield Ghost Town, Scenic Railroad, and Mine Tours—gold panning

Museums and Mine Tours
Bisbee　　Queen Mine Tour—Tour a copper mine
Flagstaff　　Meteor Crater Enterprises, Inc.—View a meteor crater, museum of astrogeology

Goldfield	Goldfield Ghost Town, Scenic Railroad, and Mine Tours—Gold mine tour, museum, ghost town
	Superstition Mountain Museum—Geology, minerals, and mining
Phoenix	Arizona Mining and Mineral Museum—3,000 minerals on exhibit, minerals from AZ copper mines, piece of meteor crater meteorite, rocks from original moon landing, spheres, fluorescent mineral display
Sun City	The Mineral Museum—3,000 rocks and minerals from the U.S. and the world, with emphasis on minerals from AZ; Over 150 fluorescent rocks and minerals, most from Franklin and Sterling Hill, NJ
Sahuarita	ASARCO Mineral Discovery Center—Geology, mining, minerals, and tour of open-pit mine
Tucson	Arizona-Sonora Desert Museum—Mineral collection from Sonoran desert region
	Mineral Museum, University of Arizona—2,100 of 15,000 minerals on display; AZ minerals, meteorites, fluorescents, borate minerals

Annual Events

Quartzite	Gem & Mineral Shows—mid-January–mid-February
Scottsdale	Minerals of Arizona—Symposium 1 day in March
Tucson	Gem & Mineral Shows—first 2 weeks in February

ARKANSAS

Fee Dig Mines and Guide Services

Hot Springs	Coleman's Crystal Mines—Dig for quartz crystals
Jessieville	Jim Coleman Crystal Mines—Dig for quartz crystals
Mt. Ida	Fiddler's Ridge Rock Shop and Crystal Mines—Dig for quartz crystals
	Leatherhead Quartz Mining—Dig for quartz crystals
	Robbin's Mining Company—Dig for quartz crystals
	Sonny Stanley's Crystal Mine—Dig for quartz crystals
	Starfire Mine—Dig for quartz crystals
	Sweet Surrender Crystal Mine—Dig for quartz crystals
	Wegner's Crystal Mine—Dig for quartz crystals
Murfreesboro	Crater of Diamonds State Park—Dig and screen for diamonds, amethyst, agates, barite, calcite, jasper, quartz, other gems
Paron	Willis Crystal Mine and Gift Shop—Dig for quartz crystals

Museums and Mine Tours

Fayetteville The University Museum—Quartz and other AR minerals
Little Rock Geology Learning Center—AR gems, minerals, fossil fuels
State University A.S.U. Museum—Minerals, many from AR

Annual Events

Mt. Ida Quartz Crystal Festival and World Championship Dig—Second weekend in October

CALIFORNIA

Fee Dig Mines and Guide Services

Angels Camp Jensen's Pick & Shovel Ranch—Guided prospecting for gold
Coloma Marshall Gold Digging State Historic Park—Gold panning
Columbia Hidden Treasures Gold Mine Tours—Gold panning
Jackson Kennedy Gold Mine—Gold panning
Lakeport Lake County Visitors Information Center—Search for Lake County "diamonds" or "moon tears"
Mariposa Little Valley Inn—Gold panning
Nevada City Malakoff Diggins State Historic Park—Gold panning
Palo Verde Opal Hill Fire Agate Mine—Dig for fire agate, micromount crystals, apatite, barite, calcite, clinoptilolite, fluorite, gypsum (curved)
Pine Grove Roaring Camp Mining Co.—Pan for gold, rockhounding
Placerville Gold Bug Mine and Hangtown's Gold Bug Park—Gold panning

Museums and Mine Tours

Allegany Underground Gold Miners Tours and Museum—Tour an active gold mine
Angels Camp Angels Camp Museum—Rocks and minerals; gold stamping mill, mining equipment
Avalon Catalina Island Museum Society Inc.—Exhibits on mining on Catalina Island
Boron Borax Global Visitors Center—Story of borax
Boron Twenty Mule Team Museum—History of area borate mining
Coloma Marshall Gold Discovery State Historic Park—Gold mining exhibit/museum
Columbia Hidden Treasure Gold Mine—Tour of active gold mine
Death Valley Furnace Creek Borax Museum—Rocks and minerals, featuring borax minerals

El Cajon	Heritage of the Americas Museum—Rocks, minerals, and meteorites
Fallbrook	Fallbrook Gem & Mineral Museum—Gems and minerals
Grass Valley	Empire Mine State Historic Park—Hardrock gold mine
Independence	Eastern California Museum—Exhibit depicts local mining
Jackson	Amador County Museum—Collection of mineral spheres from CA, UT, NV
	Kennedy Gold Mine Tours—Surface tour of gold mine
Julian	Eagle and High Peak Gold Mine Tours—Hardrock gold mine tour
	Julian Pioneer Museum—Rock and mineral display, gold mining tools and equipment displays
Lakeport	Lake County Museum—Minerals and gems from Lake County, CA
Los Angeles	Natural History Museum of Los Angeles County—52,000 specimens; minerals of CA; native gold, gems, and minerals
Mariposa	California State Mining and Mineral Museum—Gold from CA, gems and minerals from around the world
Needles	Needles Regional Museum—Needles blue agate, Colorado River pebble terrace stones
Nevada City	Malakoff Diggins State Historic Park—History of hydraulic gold mining
Pacific Grove	Pacific Grove Museum of Natural History—Monterey County rocks, fluorescent minerals
Paso Robles	El Paso des Robles Area Pioneer Museum—Display of local minerals
Placerville	Gold Bug Mine and Hangtown's Gold Bug Park—Tour hardrock gold mine
Quincy	Plumas County Museum—Exhibits on silver and copper mining in Plumas County
Rancho Palo Verdes	Point Vicente Interpretive Center—Exhibits on area geology
Redlands	San Bernardino County Museum—45,000 rocks, minerals, and gems
Ridgecrest	Maturango Museum—Small but well-rounded regional gem and mineral collection
Riverside	Jurupa Mountains Cultural Center—Crestmore minerals display, minerals from around the world on display and for sale, family education programs
	Riverside Municipal Museum—Rocks, minerals, gems, and regional geology
	World Museum of Natural History—Fluorescent minerals, meteorites, tektites, over 1,300 mineral spheres
San Diego	San Diego Natural History Museum—26,000 mineral specimens, includes minerals found in San Diego County mines

Santa Barbara	Department of Geological Sciences, U.C.S.B.—Gem and mineral collection, minerals and their tectonic settings
Shoshone	Shoshone Museum—Rock collection reflecting the geology of the area
Sierra City	Kentucky Mine and Museum—Exhibits of local gold and mercury mining
Sonora	Tuolomne County Museum—Gold from local mines
Yermo	Calico Ghost Town—Explore a silver mine
Yreka	Siskiyou County Courthouse—Gold exhibit
Yucca Valley	Hi-Desert Nature Museum—Rock and mineral collection, includes fluorescent minerals

Annual Events

Boron	Rock Bonanza—weekend before Easter
Coloma	Marshall Gold Discovery State Historic Park: Gold Rush Days—end of September–beginning of October

COLORADO

Fee Dig Mines and Guide Services

Idaho Springs	Argo Gold Mill—Pan for gold and gemstones
	Phoenix Mine—Pan for gold
Lake George (Tarryall)	Topaz Mountain Gem Mine—Screen for topaz, phenakite crystals in topaz, goshenite, quartz, feldspar

Museums and Mine Tours

Denver	Denver Museum of Natural History—2,000 specimens, includes gold, topaz, aquamarine, amazonite, and other Colorado minerals
Georgetown	Lebanon Silver Mine—Tour a silver mine
Golden	Geology Museum, Colorado School of Mines—50,000 specimens, minerals from Colorado and from around the world, gemstones and precious metals, cave exhibit
Idaho Springs	Argo Gold Mill—Historic gold mill, mining museum, Double Eagle Gold Mine
	Edgar Experimental Mine—Tour an experimental mine (silver, gold, lead, copper)
	Phoenix Mine—See a working underground hardrock mine (gold, silver)
Leadville	Matchless Mine—Tour a gold mine
	National Mining Hall of Fame and Museum—Story of the American mining industry from coal to gold

Silverton   Mayflower Gold Mill—Tour a gold mill
                   Old Hundred Gold Mine Tour, Inc.—Gold mine tour
                   San Juan County Historical Museum—Minerals and gems from the
                   Silverton area

CONNECTICUT

Fee Dig Mines and Guide Services
            None

Museums and Mine Tours
East Granby   Old New-Gate Prison and Copper Mine—Tour an old copper mine
Greenwich   Bruce Museum of Arts and Science—Minerals and rocks
New Haven   Peabody Museum of Natural History—Minerals of New England and
                  the world

DELAWARE

Fee Dig Mines and Guide Services
            None

Museums and Mine Tours
Newark   Delaware Academy of Science, Iron Hill Museum—DE minerals, flu-
                  orescent minerals
                  University of Delaware, Mineralogical Museum—5,000 specimens
                  (1,000 on display), crystals, gems, minerals

DISTRICT OF COLUMBIA

Fee Dig Mines and Guide Services
            None

Museums and Mine Tours
            Smithsonian Institution, National Museum of Natural History—
            Gems and minerals

FLORIDA

Fee Dig Mines and Guide Services
            None

Museums and Mine Tours

Mulberry   Mulberry Phosphate Museum—Exhibits on the phosphate industry

Tampa   Ed and Bernadette Marcin Museum, University of Florida—Minerals and gemstones mainly from FL and the western U.S.

GEORGIA

Fee Dig Mines and Guide Services

Cleveland   Gold'n Gem Grubbin—Dig and pan for gold, sapphires, rubies, emeralds, amethyst, topaz

Dahlonega   Consolidated Gold Mine—Gold panning

Crisson Gold Mine—Pan gold sands or enriched gemstone ore

Helen   Gold Mine of Helen, GA—Pan gold sand or enriched gemstone ore

Lincolnton   Graves Mountain—Search for audite, lazulite, pyrophyllite, kyanite, hematite, pyrite, ilmenite, muscovite, fuchsite, barite, sulfur, blue quartz, quartz crystals, microcrystals such as woodhouseite, variscite, strengite, phosphosiderite, cacoxenite, crandallite

Museums and Mine Tours

Atlanta   Fernbank Museum of Natural History—Joachim gem collection containing 400 cut and polished gemstones

Fernbank Science Center—Gems, carved opals, meteorites

Cartersville   William Weinman Mineral Museum—2,000 specimens, gems and minerals from the state; simulated cave

Dahlonega   Consolidated Gold Mine—Mine tour

Dahlonega Gold Museum—Tells the story of the GA Gold Rush

Elberton   Elberton Granite Museum—Granite quarry and products

Helen   Gold Mine of Helen, GA—Mine tour

Macon   Museum of Arts and Science—Display of gems and minerals

Statesboro   Georgia Southern Museum—Collection of rocks and minerals from Georgia's highlands, Piedmont, and coastal regions

Tallapoosa   West Georgia Museum of Tallapoosa—Small collection of local minerals

Annual Events

Jasper   Pickens County Marble Festival—First weekend in October

HAWAII

Fee Dig Mines and Guide Services
None

Museums and Mine Tours
Hawaii Nat'l Park Thomas A. Jaggar Museum—Museum on vulcanology and seismology; tour of volcano

Hilo Lyman House Memorial Museum—Rocks, minerals, gems

IDAHO

Fee Dig Mines and Guide Services
Moscow 3-D's Panhandle Gems and Garnet Queen Mine—Guide service, star garnet digging; trips including gold panning.

Spencer Spencer Opal Mine—Pick through a stockpile for fire opal; pre-arranged digging at mine is a possibility

St. Maries Emerald Creek Garnet Area—Dig for star garnets

Museums and Mine Tours
Caldwell The Glen L. and Ruth M. Evans Gem and Mineral Collection—Agate, jasper, other gemstones, 2,000 cabochons

Orma J. Smith Museum of Natural History—Extensive collection of minerals

ILLINOIS

Fee Dig Mines and Guide Services
None

Museums and Mine Tours
Chicago The Field Museum—92-year-old gem exhibit

Elmhurst Lizzadro Museum of Lapidary Art—1,300 pieces of cut and polished gems, fluorescent rocks, a birthstone display

Galena Vinegar Hill Lead Mine and Museum—Mine tour and museum

Rock Island Augustana Fryxell Geology Museum—Rock and mineral musuem

Rosiclare The American Fluorite Museum—Story of Fluorospur Industry

Springfield Illinois State Museum—Gems and minerals, Illinois specimens, birthstones, fluorescents, copper

West Frankfort The National Coal Museum, Mine 25—Tour a shaft coal mine

INDIANA

Fee Dig Mines and Guide Services
Knightstown   Yogi Bear Jellystone Park Camping Resort—Midwestern gold prospecting

Museums and Mine Tours
Bedford   Land of Limestone Exhibition—History of Indiana Limestone industry

Fort Wayne   Indiana Purdue University at Fort Wayne—Hallway displays of minerals, meteorites, and rocks

Indianapolis   Indiana State Museum—Indiana and regional minerals

Richmond   Joseph Moore Museum of Natural History, Earlham College—Geology exhibit from local Ordovician limestone

IOWA

Fee Dig Mines and Guide Services
None

Museums and Mine Tours
Danville   Geode State Park—Display of geodes

Iowa City   University of Iowa—Displays on state geology

Sioux City   Sioux City Public Museum—Mineralogy exhibit

Waterloo   Grout Museum—Display of rocks and minerals

West Bend   Grotto of the Redemption—Grotto made of precious stones and gems

Winterset   Madison County Historical Society—Rock and mineral collection

KANSAS

Fee Dig Mines and Guide Services
None

Museums and Mine Tours
Ashland   Pioneer Krier Museum—Mineral exhibit

Greensburg   Pallasite Meteorite at the Big Well Museum—Meteorite strike site and 1,000-pound meteorite

McPherson   McPherson Museum—Meteorites

KENTUCKY

Fee Dig Mines and Guide Services
> None

Museums and Mine Tours

Benham   Kentucky Coal Mine Museum—Displays on coal mining and forma-
             tion of coal
Covington   Behringen-Crawford Museum—Display of gems and minerals
Lynch   Lynch Portal 31 Walking Tour—Walking tour of coal mining facili-
             ties
Marion   The Clement Mineral Museum—Display of gems and minerals

LOUISIANA

Fee Dig Mines and Guide Services
> None

Museums and Mine Tours

New Orleans Louisiana Nature Center—Small collection of gems and minerals
Shreveport   Louisiana State Exhibit Museum—Displays on mining and salt
             domes

MAINE

Fee Dig Mines and Guide Services

Albany   Bumpus Quarry—Collect garnet, albite, beryl, rose quartz, and black
             tourmaline
Bethel   Songo Pond Mine—Collect tourmaline and other ME gems and min-
             erals
Poland   Poland Mining Camp—Collect tourmaline and other ME gems and
             minerals
West Paris   Perham's of West Paris—Collect tourmaline and other ME gems and
             minerals

Museums and Mine Tours

Augusta   Maine State Museum—Gems and minerals of ME
West Paris   Perham's of West Paris—ME gems and minerals; model of a feldspar
             quarry, model of a gem tourmaline pocket, fluorescents

Annual Events

Augusta   Maine Mineral Symposium—3rd weekend in May

MARYLAND

Fee Dig Mines and Guide Services
> None

Museums and Mine Tours
> None

MASSACHUSETTS

Fee Dig Mines and Guide Services
> None

Museums and Mine Tours

Amherst — Pratt Museum of Natural History—10,000 specimens; minerals from New England and around the world, meteorites

Cambridge — Harvard University Museum of Cultural and Natural History— Gems, minerals, ores, meteorites

Springfield — Springfield Science Museum—Minerals from around the world

MICHIGAN

Fee Dig Mines and Guide Services

Mohawk — Delaware Copper Mine—Search for souvenir copper

Museums and Mine Tours

Ann Arbor — Exhibit Museum of Natural History, University of Michigan— Exhibits of rocks and minerals

Bloomfield Hills Cranbrook Institute of Science—5,000 minerals and crystals from around the world, including hiddenite, gold

Calumet — Mining Museum at Coppertown, U.S.A.—Exhibits on copper mining

Caspian — Iron County Museum and Park—Iron mining complex

Chelsea — Gerald E. Eddy Geology Center—MI rocks, minerals, crystals, and mining

Copper Harbor Fort Wilkins State Park—History of copper mining in the area

Hancock — The Quincy Mining Company—Tour an underground copper mine

Houghton — The Seaman Mineral Museum—Crystal collection, minerals from the Lake Superior copper district

Iron Mountain Iron Mountain Iron Mine—Iron mine tour

Lake Linden — Houghton County Historical Museum—Copper mining and refining equipment displays

Mohawk	Delaware Copper Mine—Mine tour
Mount Pleasant	Museum of Cultural and Natural History, Central Michigan University—MI rocks and minerals
Negaunee	Michigan Iron Industry Museum—Story of MI iron industry
Shelby	Shelby Man-Made Gemstones—Exhibits on producing artificial gems

MINNESOTA

Fee Dig Mines and Guide Services
None

Museums and Mine Tours
Calumet	Hill Annex Mine State Park—Tour an open pit iron mine
Chisholm	Ironworld Discovery Center—Iron industry taconite mining tours
	Minnesota Museum of Mining—Indoor and outdoor exhibits
	Taconite Mine Tours—Tour of an open-pit iron ore mine
Hibbing	Mahoning Hull-Rust Mine—Observe an open-pit iron mine
Pipestone	Pipestone National Monument—Tour a Native American pipestone quarry
Soudan	Soudan Underground Mine State Park—Tour an underground iron mine
Virginia	Mineview in the Sky—View an open-pit iron ore mine
	Iron Trails Conventions and Visitor's Bureau—Information on mine view sites

MISSISSIPPI

Fee Dig Mines and Guide Services
None

Museums and Mine Tours
| Greenwood | Cottonlandia Museum—Rocks and minerals from around the world |

MISSOURI

Fee Dig Mines and Guide Services
| Alexandria | Sheffler Rock Shop—Dig geodes lined with crystals |

Museums and Mine Tours

Golden	Golden Pioneer Museum—Large mineral exhibit
Joplin	Everett J. Richie Tri-State Mineral Museum—Story of area's lead and zinc mining
Kansas City	University of Missouri–Kansas City, Geosciences Museum—Local and regional specimens
Park Hills	Missouri Mines State Historic Site—1,100 minerals, ores, and rocks
Point Lookout	Ralph Foster Museum, College of the Ozarks—Gemstone spheres and fluorescent minerals
Rolla	Mineral Museum, U. of Missouri, Rolla—3,500 minerals, ores, and rocks from 92 countries and 47 states

MONTANA

Fee Dig Mines and Guide Services

Alder	Red Rock Mine—Screen for garnets
Clinton	L◊E Guest Ranch Outfitters—Sapphire mining pack trips
Dillon	Crystal Park Recreational Mineral Collecting Area—Dig for quartz and amethyst crystal
Hamilton	Sapphire Studio—Sapphire mining "parties"
Helena	Spokane Bar Sapphire Mine and Gold Fever Rock Shop—Dig and screen for sapphires and other gems and minerals
Philipsburg	Gem Mountain—search for sapphires
	Sapphire Gallery—Wash bags of gravel to look for sapphires

Museums and Mine Tours

Butte	Anselmo Mine Yard—Tour of mining facilities and history of area mining
	The Berkeley Pit—Observation point for closed open-pit copper mine
	Butte-Silver Bow Visitors and Transportation Center—Presents information on area geology and its mining, including local gold and silver mining
	Mineral Museum, Montana College of Mineral Science and Technology—Gold, fluorescents, and minerals from Butte and MT
	World Museum of Mining and 1899 Mining Camp—Tour of surface facilities of former silver and zinc mine
Ekalaka	Carter County Museum—Fluorescent mineral display
Lewistown	Central Montana Museum—Rocks, minerals, and yogo sapphires

NEBRASKA

Fee Dig Mines and Guide Services
>None

Museums and Mine Tours

Hastings   Hastings Museum—Minerals, rocks, fluorescent minerals, and translucent slabs

Lincoln   University of Nebraska State Museum—Displays of rocks, minerals and fluorescent rocks

NEVADA

Fee Dig Mines and Guide Services

Denio   Rainbow Ridge Opal Mine—Tailings digging for wood opal

Royal Peacock Opal Mine, Inc.—Dig black and fire opal

Ely   Garnet Fields Rockhound Area—Hunt for garnets

Gerlach   Royal Rainbow Fire Opal Mine—Dig for fire opal

Museums and Mine Tours

Las Vegas   Nevada State Museum and Historical Society—Natural history of Nevada

Virginia City   Chollar Mine—Underground mine tour (gold and silver mine)

NEW HAMPSHIRE

Fee Dig Mines and Guide Services

Grafton   Ruggles Mine—Collect up to 150 different minerals

Museums and Mine Tours

Dover   The Woodman Institute—1,300 specimens, including local rocks

NEW JERSEY

Fee Dig Mines and Guide Services

Cape May   Cape May Welcome Center—Hunt for Cape May "diamonds"

Franklin   Franklin Mineral Museum and Buckwheat Dump—Tailings diggings for fluorescent minerals

Museums and Mine Tours

Franklin   Franklin Mineral Museum—Minerals, rocks, local and worldwide fluorescents

Monroe Township	Displayworld's Stone Museum—Minerals, hands-on exhibits
Morristown	Morristown Museum—Specimens from five continents
New Brunswick	Rutgers Geology Museum—Specimens from the zinc deposit at Franklin and the zeolite deposits from Paterson, meteorites
Ogdensburg	Sterling Hill Mine and Museum—Tour old zinc mine
Paterson	The Paterson Museum—Specimens from local basalt flows and basalt flow in the Poona region of India, minerals from NJ and around the world
Rutherford	Meadowland Museum—Fluorescent minerals, quartz, minerals from NJ
Trenton	New Jersey State Museum—Minerals and rocks, including fluorescents and magnetite ore

Annual Events

| Franklin | New Jersey Earth Science Association Gem and Mineral Show and Outdoor Swap & Sell—Late April |

NEW MEXICO

Fee Dig Mines and Guide Services

Bingham	Blanchard Mines—Collect over 84 different kinds of minerals in a former lead mine
Deming	Rockhound State Park—collect a variety of semiprecious stones
Dixon	Harding Mine—Harding pegmatite has yielded over 50 minerals
Magdalena	Bill's Gems & Minerals—Collect copper and iron minerals at mine dumps

Museums and Mine Tours

Albuquerque	Geology Museum, University of New Mexico—Displays of NM minerals and geology
	Institute of Meteoritics, University of New Mexico—Meteorites
	New Mexico Museum of Natural History and Science—3,000 specimens with a focus on NM and the southwestern U.S.
	The Turquoise Museum—Turquoise museum
Socorro	New Mexico Bureau of Mines and Mineral Resources—10,000 specimens of minerals from NM, the U.S., and the world

Annual Events

| Socorro | New Mexico Mineral Symposium |

NEW YORK

Fee Dig Mines and Guide Services

Herkimer	Herkimer Diamond Mine and KOA Kampground—Dig for Herkimer "Diamonds"
Little Falls	Treasure Mountain Diamond Mine—Dig for Herkimer "Diamonds"
Middleville	Ace of Diamonds Mine and Campground—Prospect for Herkimer "Diamonds"
North River	Barton Mines—Hunt for garnets
St. Johnsville	Crystal Grove Diamond Mine and Campground—Dig for Herkimer "Diamonds"

Museums and Mine Tours

Albany	New York State Museum—Minerals from New York
Hicksville	The Hicksville Gregory Museum—9,000 specimens form the major minerals groups; also NJ zeolites, Herkimer "diamonds," fluorescents
New York	American Museum of Natural History—Gems, meteorites; emphasis on exceptional specimens from the U.S.
Pawling	The Gunnison Natural History Museum—Minerals

NORTH CAROLINA

Fee Dig Mines and Guide Services

Almond	Nantahala Gorge Ruby Mine—Sluice for rubies, sapphires, amethyst, topaz, garnet, citrine, smoky quartz
Canton	Old Pressley Sapphire Mine—Sluice for sapphires
Cherokee	Smoky Mountain Gold & Ruby Mine—Sluice for gold and gems
Franklin	Cherokee Ruby and Sapphire Mine—Sluice for rubies, sapphires, garnets, moonstones, rutile, sillimanite
	Cowee Mountain Ruby Mine—Sluice for rubies, sapphires, garnets, tourmaline, smoky quartz, amethyst, citrine, moonstone, topaz
	Gold City Gem Mine—Sluice for rubies, sapphires, garnets, emeralds, tourmaline, smoky quartz, amethyst, citrine, moonstone, topaz
	Jackson Hole—Sluice for rubies, sapphire, garnets, tourmaline, smoky quartz, amethyst, citrine, moonstone, topaz
	Mason Mountain Rhodolite and Ruby Mine and Cowee Gift Shop—Sluice for rhodolite, rubies, sapphires, garnets, kyanite, crystal quartz, smoky quartz, moonstones
	Masons Ruby and Sapphire Mine—Dig and sluice for sapphires (all colors), pink and red rubies

Moonstone Gem Mine—Sluice for rhodolite, rubies, sapphires, garnets, other precious stones

The Old Cardinal Gem Mine—Sluice for rare native rhodolite, rubies, sapphires, garnets, moonstones, topaz, other precious stones

Rocky Face Gem Mine—Sluice for rubies, rhodolite garnets

Rose Creek Mine, Campground, Trout Pond, and Rock Shop—Sluice for rubies, sapphires, garnets, moonstones, amethysts, smoky quartz, citrine, rose quartz, topaz

Sheffield Mine—Sluice for rubies, sapphires, enriched material from around the world

Hiddenite   Emerald Hollow Mine, Hiddenite Gems, Inc.—Rutile, sapphires, garnets, monazite, hiddenite, smoky quartz, tourmaline, clear quartz, aquamarine, sillimanite

Little Switzerland   Blue Ridge Gemstone Mine & Campground—Sapphire, emeralds, rubies, aquamarine, tourmaline, topaz, garnets, amethysts, lepidolite, citrine, moonstone, kyanite, and rose, clear, rutilated, and smoky quartz

Emerald Village—Sapphire, emeralds, rubies, aquamarine, tourmaline, topaz, garnets, amethysts, lepidolite, citrine, beryl, moonstone, kyanite, and rose, clear, rutilated, and smoky quartz

Marion   The Lucky Strike—Gems and gold panning

Carolina Emerald Mine and Vein Mountain Gold Camp—Mine for gold, emerald, aquamarine, moonstone, feldspar crystals, garnets, smoky, rose, blue and clear quartz, and tourmaline

New London   Cotton Patch Gold Mine—Gold panning

Spruce Pine   Gem Mountain Gemstone Mine—Sapphires, crabtree emeralds, rubies, Wiseman aquamarine

Rio Doce Gem Mine—Sapphires, emeralds, rubies, aquamarine, tourmaline, topaz, garnets, amethysts, lepidolite, citrine, beryl, moonstone, kyanite, and rose, clear, rutilated, and smoky quartz

Rock Mine Tours and Gift Shop—Dig for emeralds, aquamarine, golden beryl, feldspar, pink feldspar, star garnets, biotite, olivine, moonstone, thulite, and black tourmaline

Spruce Pine Gem and Gold Mine—Sapphires, emeralds, rubies, aquamarine, tourmaline, topaz, garnets, amethysts, lepidolite, citrine, beryl, moonstone, kyanite, and rose, clear, rutilated, and smoky quartz

Stanfield   Reed Gold Mine Historic Site—Gold panning

Union Mills   Thermal City Gold Mining Company—Gold panning

Museums and Mine Tours

Asheville   Colburn Gem & Mineral Museum—Collection of mineral specimens from NC and the world

Franklin	Franklin Gem and Mineral Museum—Specimens from NC and around the world
	Ruby City Gems—Specimens from NC and around the world
Gastonia	Schiele Museum—North Carolina gems and minerals
Greensboro	Natural Science Center of Greensboro—Specimens from NC and around the world
Hendersonville	Mineral and Lapidary Museum of Hendersonville, Inc.—Minerals and lapidary arts
Linville	Grandfather Mountain Nature Museum—Specimens from NC
Little Switzerland	North Carolina Mining Museum and Mine Tour—tour a closed feldspar mine
Spruce Pine	Museum of North Carolina Minerals—Specimens primarily from local mines
Stanfield	Reed Gold Mine Historic Site—Gold mine tour

Annual Events

Franklin	Macon County Gemboree—3rd weekend in July
	"Leaf Looker" Gemboree—2nd weekend in October
Spruce Pine	Original NC Mineral and Gem Festival—4 days at the beginning of August

NORTH DAKOTA

Fee Dig Mines and Guide Services
None

Museums and Mine Tours
Dickinson	Dakota Dinosaur Museum—Rocks and minerals, including borax from CA, turquoise from AZ, fluorescents, aurora crystals from AR

OHIO

Fee Dig Mines and Guide Services
Hopewell	Hidden Springs Ranch—Dig for flint (groups only)
	Nethers Flint—Dig for flint

Museums and Mine Tours
Cleveland	The Cleveland Museum of Natural History—The Wade Gallery of Gems and Minerals has over 1,500 gems and minerals

Columbus	Orton Geological Museum—Rocks and minerals from OH and the world
Dayton	Boonshoft Museum of Discovery—Minerals and crystals
Glenford	Flint Ridge State Memorial—Ancient flint quarrying
Lima	Allen County Museum—Rock and mineral exhibit

OKLAHOMA

Fee Dig Mines and Guide Services

Jet	Salt Plains National Wildlife Refuge—Digging for selenite crystals
Kenton	Black Mesa Bed & Breakfast—Rockhounding on a working cattle ranch
	Howard Layton Ranch—Rockhounding on a working cattle ranch

Museums and Mine Tours

Coalgate	Coal Country Mining and Historical Museum—Mining museum
Enid	The Mr. and Mrs. Dan Midgley Museum—Rock and mineral collection predominantly from OK and the TX shoreline
Noble	Timberlake Rose Rock Museum—Displays of barite roses
Picher	Picher Mining Museum—Lead and zinc mining
Tulsa	Elsing Museum—Gems and minerals

Annual Events

| Cherokee | The Crystal Festival and Selenite Crystal Dig—First Saturday in May |
| Noble | Annual Rose Rock Festival—First Saturday in May |

OREGON

Fee Dig Mines and Guide Services

Madras	Richards Recreational Ranch—Dig for thundereggs, agate
Mitchell	Lucky Strike Geodes—Dig for thundereggs (picture jasper)
Yachats	Beachcombing—Collect agates and jaspers

Museums and Mine Tours

Central Point	Crater Rock Museum—Minerals, thundereggs, fossils, geodes, cut and polished gemstones
Redmond	Peterson's Rock Garden—Unusual rock specimens, fluorescent display
Sumpter	Sumpter Valley Dredge State Historical Heritage Area—View a gold dredge, tour historic gold mine towns

Annual Events

Cottage Grove Bohemia Mining Days—Four days in July, gold panning and exposition
Prineville Rockhounds Pow-Wow—mid-June

PENNSYLVANIA

Fee Dig Mines and Guide Services
    None

Museums and Mine Tours

Ashland Museum of Anthracite Mining—Story of anthracite coal
Pioneer Tunnel Coal Mine—Tour an anthracite coal mine

Bryn Mawr Museum, Department of Geology, Bryn Mawr College—Rotating display of 1,500 minerals from collection of 23,500 specimens

Carlisle Rennie Geology Museum, Dickinson College—Gem and mineral display

Harrisburg State Museum of Pennsylvania—Geology of everyday products

Lancaster North Museum of Natural History and Science—Worldwide specimens with a focus on Lancaster County

Media Delaware County Institute of Science—Minerals from around the world

Patton Seldom Seen Mine—Tour a bituminous coal mine

Philadelphia Wagner Free Institute of Science—Rocks and minerals

Pittsburgh Carnegie Museum of Natural History—Gems and minerals

Scranton Anthracite Museum Complex—Several anthracite coal–related attractions, including mine tours and museums

Tarentum Tour-Ed Mine—Bituminous coal mine tour

University Park College of Earth and Mineral Sciences, Penn State University—Minerals

Waynesburg Paul R. Stewart Museum, Waynesburg College—Outstanding mineral collection

West Chester Geology Museum, West Chester University—Specimens from Chester County, fluorescent specimens

Wilkes-Barre Wyoming Historical & Geological Society Museum—Displays on anthracite coal mining

Windber Windber Coal Heritage Center—Exhibits present the heritage of coal mining

Annual Events

Pittsburgh The Carnegie Museum of Natural History Gem & Mineral Show—last weekend in August

University Park Mineral Symposium—Three days in May

RHODE ISLAND

Fee Dig Mines and Guide Services
> None

Museums and Mine Tours

Providence Museum of Natural History and Planetarium—Rocks and minerals

SOUTH CAROLINA

Fee Dig Mines and Guide Services
> None

Museums and Mine Tours

Charleston Charleston Museum—Small display of gems and minerals

Clemson Bob Campbell Geology Museum—Minerals, meteorites, faceted stones

Columbia McKissick Museum, University of South Carolina Campus—Exhibits on geology and gemstones

South Carolina State Museum—Small display of rocks and minerals

SOUTH DAKOTA

Fee Dig Mines and Guide Services

Deadwood Broken Boot Gold Mine—Pan for gold

Keystone Big Thunder Gold Mine—Pan for gold

Lead Black Hills Mining Museum—Pan for gold

Wall Buffalo Gap National Grasslands—Hunt for agates

Museums and Mine Tours

Deadwood Broken Boot Gold Mine—Gold mine tour

Keystone Big Thunder Gold Mine—Underground mine tour

Lead Black Hills Mining Museum—Simulated underground mine tour

Homestead Visitors Center—Gold mining displays

Murdo National Rockhound and Lapidary Hall of Fame—Gems and minerals

Rapid City South Dakota School of Mines and Technology—Local minerals

TENNESSEE

Fee Dig Mines and Guide Services
Ducktown   Burra Burra Mine—Dig for garnets, pyrite, chalcopyrite, pyrrhotite, actinolite

Museums and Mine Tours
Johnson City   Hands On! Regional Museum—Simulated coal mine
Knoxville   McClung Museum—Geology of Tennessee
Memphis   Memphis Pink Palace Museum—Geology and minerals from famous mid-South localities

TEXAS

Fee Dig Mines and Guide Services
Alpine   Stillwell Ranch—Hunt for agate and jasper
  Woodward Ranch—Hunt for agate, precious opal, and others
Mason   Hoffman Ranch—Hunt for topaz
  Seaquist Ranch—Hunt for topaz
Three Rivers   House Ranch—Hunt for agate

Museums and Mine Tours
Austin   Texas Memorial Museum—Gems and minerals
Canyon   Panhandle Plains Historical Museum—Gems and minerals from the TX panhandle; meteorites
Fort Stockton   Annie Riggs Memorial Museum—Rocks and minerals of Pecos County and the Big Bend area
Fritch   Alibates Flint Quarries—View ancient flint quarries
Marble Falls   Granite Mountain—View marble mining operations
McKinney   The Heard Natural Science Museum and Wildlife Sanctuary—Rocks and minerals
Odessa   Odessa Meteor Crater—Meteorite crater

Annual Events
Alpine   Alpine Gem Show—mid-April

UTAH

Fee Dig Mines and Guide Services
  None

Museums and Mine Tours

Bingham Canyon	Bingham Canyon Mine Visitors Center—Overlook for open-pit-copper mine
Eureka	Tintec Mining Museum—Mineral display and mining artifacts
Helper	Western Mining and Railroad Museum—Mining exhibits, simulated 1900 coal mine
Hyrum	Hyrum City Museum—Display of fluorescent minerals
Lehi	John Hutchings Museum of Natural History—Minerals linked to mining districts, display of uncut gems
Salt Lake City	Utah Museum of Natural History—Mineral classification; UT ores and minerals, fluorescent minerals

VERMONT

Fee Dig Mines and Guide Services

None

Museums and Mine Tours

Barre	Rock of Ages Corporation—Watch granite being quarried
Norwich	Montshire Museum of Science—Fluorescent minerals
Proctor	Vermont Marble Exhibit—Story of marble

VIRGINIA

Fee Dig Mines and Guide Services

Amelia	Dick R. Boyles—Dig for beryl
	Morefield Gem Mine—Dig and sluice for garnet, quartz, topaz, and many others
Stuart	Fairy Stone State Park—Hunt for staurolite crystals (fairy stones)

Museums and Mine Tours

Blocksburg	Virginia Tech Museum of Geological Sciences—Large display of Virginia minerals
Martinsville	Virginia Museum of Natural History—Minerals and mining exhibits

WASHINGTON

Fee Dig Mines and Guide Services

Ravensdale	Bob Jackson's Geology Adventures—Field trips: collect quartz, garnets, topaz, and others

Museums and Mine Tours

Castle Rock   Mount St. Helens National Volcanic Monument—Focus on geology
Ellensburg   Kittitas County Historical Museum and Society—Polished rocks
Pullman   Washington State University—Silicified wood, minerals
Seattle   Burke Museum of Natural History and Culture—Rocks, minerals, the geology of Washington, and a walk-through volcano

WEST VIRGINIA

Fee Dig Mines and Guide Services
None

Museums and Mine Tours
Beckley   The Beckley Exhibition Coal Mine—Tour a bituminous coal mine

WISCONSIN

Fee Dig Mines and Guide Services
None

Museums and Mine Tours
Dodgeville   The Museum of Minerals and Crystals—Local mineral specimens, specimens from around the world
Hurley   Iron County Historical Museum—History of area mining, also, last remaining mine head frame in Wisconsin
Madison   Geology Museum, University of Wisconsin at Madison—Minerals, fluorescent minerals, model of Wisconsin cave
Milwaukee   Milwaukee Public Museum—Displays of geological specimens
University of Wisconsin at Milwaukee—Minerals
Platteville   The Mining Museum—Lead and zinc mining in the upper Mississippi Valley
Stevens Point   Museum of Natural History—University of Wisconsin—Stevens Point rock and mineral display

WYOMING

Fee Dig Mines and Guide Services
Shell   Trapper Galloway Ranch—Dig for moss agate

Museums and Mine Tours
Casper   Tate Geological Museum—Rocks and minerals, including WY jade, and fluorescent minerals

Cheyenne	Wyoming State Museum—Minerals of Wyoming, coal "Swamp"
Laramie	Geological Museum, University of Wyoming—Rocks and minerals, fluorescent minerals from WY
Rock River	Rock River Museum—Fluorescent mineral display
Saritoga	Saritoga Museum—Minerals from around the world, local geology
Worland	Washaki Museum—Agates, crystals

Annual Events

Casper	Tate Geological Museum Symposium on Wyoming Geology—June

Index by Gems and Minerals

This index lists all the gems and minerals that can be found at fee dig mines in the U.S., and shows the city and state where the mine is located. To use the index, look up the gem or mineral you are interested in, and note the states and cities where they are located. Then go to the state and city to find the name of the mine, and information about the mine.

The following notes provide additional information:

(#)   A number in parentheses is the number of mines in that town that have that gem or mineral.

(*)   Gem or mineral is found in the state, but the mine may also add material to the ore. Check with the individual mine for confirmation.

(FT)   Field trip.

(GS)   Guide service (location listed is the location of the guide service, not necessarily the location of the gems or minerals being collected).

(I)   Mineral has been identified at the mine site but may be difficult to find.

(M)   Museum that allows collection of one specimen as a souvenir.

(MM)   Micromount (a very small crystal which, when viewed under a microscope or magnifying glass, is found to be a high-quality crystal).

(O)   Available at mine but comes from other mines.

(R)   Can be found, but is rare.

(S)   Not the main gem or mineral for which the site is known.

(SA)   "Salted" or enriched gem or mineral.

(U)   Unique to the site.

(Y)   Yearly collecting event.

Actinolite Tennessee: Ducktown

Agate Arkansas: Murfreesboro (S); Iowa: Bonaporte; Montana: Helena (S); Nevada: Gerlach; New Mexico: Deming (GS); Oklahoma: Kenton (2); Oregon: Yachats; South Dakota: Wall; Texas: Three Rivers; Virginia: Amelia
  Banded agate Texas: Alpine
  Fire agate California: Palo Verde
  Iris agate Texas: Alpine

Ledge agate Oregon: Madras
Moss agate Oregon: Madras, Mitchell; Texas: Alpine (2); Wyoming: Shell
Polka-dot jasp-agate Oregon: Madras
Plume agate Oregon: Madras
Pompom agate Texas: Alpine
Rainbow agate Oregon: Madras
Red plume agate Texas: Alpine

Albite Maine: Albany, Poland (GS), West Paris; New Hampshire: Grafton (I); New Mexico: Dixon

Albite (Cleavelandite Var.) Maine: Poland (GS)

Amazonite Virginia: Amelia

Amber Texas: Mason (R); Washington: Ravensdale (GS)

Amethyst Arkansas: Murfreesboro (S); Georgia: Cleveland, Helen (SA); Maine: Bethel (R), West Paris; Montana: Dillon; New Hampshire: Grafton (I); New Mexico: Bingham; North Carolina (*): Almond, Cherokee, Franklin (5), Little Switzerland, Spruce Pine (3)
Crystal scepters Nevada: Sun Valley (GS)

Amblygonite Maine: West Paris

Amphibolite New Hampshire: Grafton (I)

Apatite California: Palo Verde (MM); Maine: Bethel, Poland (GS), West Paris; New Hampshire: Grafton; New Mexico, Dixon
Fluorapatite Maine: Poland (GS)
Green apatite Maine: West Paris
Hydroxylapatite Maine: Poland (GS)
Purple apatite Maine: West Paris

Aplite New Hampshire: Grafton (I)

Aquamarine Maine: Bethel, Poland (GS); New Hampshire: Grafton (I); North Carolina (*): Hiddenite, Little Switzerland (2), Marion, Spruce Pine (2) (FT)
Brushy Creek aquamarine North Carolina: Spruce Pine (1) (FT)
Weisman aquamarine North Carolina: Spruce Pine (1) (FT)

Arsenopyrite Maine: Poland (GS)

Augelite Maine: Poland (GS)

Aurichalcite New Mexico: Bingham, Magdalena

Autenite Maine: Poland (GS); New Hampshire: Grafton (I)

Azurite New Mexico: Magdalena; Utah: Moab (GS)

Barite Arkansas: Murfreesboro (S); California: Palo Verde (MM); Georgia: Lincolnton; New Mexico: Bingham; Washington: Ravensdale (GS)

Beraumite Maine: Poland (GS)

Bermanite Maine: Poland (GS)

Bertrandite Maine: Poland (GS), West Paris

Bertranite New Hampshire: Grafton (I)

Beryl Maine: Albany, Poland (GS), West Paris; New Mexico, Dixon; North Carolina (*): Little Switzerland (2), Spruce Pine (2); South Dakota: Custer (GS); Virginia: Amelia (2)
    Aqua beryl New Hampshire: Grafton (I)
    Blue beryl (see also aquamarine) New Hampshire: Grafton (I)
    Golden beryl North Carolina: Spruce Pine (FT); New Hampshire: Grafton (I)

Beryllonite Maine: Poland (GS), West Paris

Biotite New Hampshire: Grafton (I); North Carolina: Spruce Pine

Borate California: Boron (Y)

Bornite New Hampshire: Grafton (I)

Brazilianite Maine: Poland (GS)

Brochantite New Mexico: Bingham

Calcite Arkansas: Murfreesboro (S); California: Palo Verde (MM); New Hampshire: Grafton; New Mexico: Bingham; Virginia: Amelia

Cape May "diamonds" See Quartz

Casserite Maine: Poland (GS)

Cassiterite Maine: West Paris

Cerussite New Mexico: Bingham

Chalcedony New Mexico: Deming

Chalcopyrite Tennessee: Ducktown

Childrenite Maine: Poland (GS)

Chrysoberyl Maine: West Paris; New Hampshire: Grafton (I)

Chrysocolla New Mexico: Bingham

Citrine Georgia: Helen (SA); North Carolina (SA): Almond, Cherokee, Franklin (6), Little Switzerland, Spruce Pine (3)

Clarkite New Hampshire: Grafton (I)

Clevelandite Maine: West Paris; New Hampshire: Grafton (I); New Mexico: Dixon

Clinoptilolite California: Palo Verde (MM)

Columbite New Hampshire: Grafton (I); Maine: Bethel, Poland (GS), West Paris

Compotite New Hampshire: Grafton (I)

Cookeite Maine: West Paris

Copper minerals Michigan: Mohawk (M); New Mexico: Magdalena

Covellite New Mexico: Bingham

Crandalite Georgia: Lincolnton

Cryolite New Hampshire: Grafton (I)

Cuprite New Mexico: Bingham

Cymatolite New Hampshire: Grafton (I)

Dendrites Nevada: Gerlach; New Hampshire: Grafton (I)

Diadochite Maine: Poland (GS)

Diamond Arkansas: Murfreesboro

Dickinsonite Maine: Poland (GS)

Earlshannonite Maine: Poland (GS)

Elbaite See listing under Tourmaline

Emerald Georgia: Cleveland, Dahlonega (SA); North Carolina (*): Cherokee, Franklin, Hiddenite, Little Switzerland (2), Marion, Spruce Pine (2)
  Crabtree Emerald North Carolina: Spruce Pine

Eosphorite Maine: Poland (GS)

Fairfieldite Maine: Poland (GS)

Fairy stones (See Staurolite crystals)

Feldspar Colorado: Lake George; New Hampshire: Grafton (I); North Carolina: Marion, Spruce Pine; Virginia: Amelia
  Albite feldspar Maine: Bethel

Flint Ohio: Hopewell (2)

Fluoroapatite New Hampshire: Grafton (I)

Fluorescent minerals New Jersey: Franklin; North Carolina: Little Switzerland; Washington: Ravensdale (GS)

Fluorite California: Palo Verde (MM); New Mexico: Bingham, Socorro (Y); South Dakota: Custer (GS); Virginia: Amelia; Washington: Ravensdale (GS)

Gahnite (spinel) Maine: Poland (GS), West Paris

Gainsite Maine: Poland (GS)

Galena New Mexico: Bingham

Garnets Georgia: Dahlonega (SA), Helen (SA); Idaho: St. Maries; Maine: Albany, Bethel, Poland (GS), West Paris (3); Montana: Alder, Helena (S); New Hampshire: Grafton (I); New Mexico: Dixon; New York: North River; North Carolina (*): Almond, Cherokee, Franklin (7), Hiddenite, Little Switzerland (2), Marion, Spruce Pine (3) (FT); Nevada: Ely; Tennessee: Ducktown; Washington: Ravensdale (GS)
  Almandine garnets Maine: Poland (GS); Nevada: Ely
  Pyrope garnets North Carolina: Franklin
  Rhodolite garnets North Carolina: Franklin (5)
Garnets, Star Idaho: Moscow (GS), St. Maries

Geodes Missouri: Alexandria; New Mexico: Deming
Lined with:
Agate, blue New Mexico: Deming
Aragonite Missouri: Alexandria
Barites Missouri: Alexandria
Chalcedony New Mexico: Deming
Dolomite Missouri: Alexandria
Goethite Missouri: Alexandria
Hematite Missouri: Alexandria
Kaoline Missouri: Alexandria
Opal, common New Mexico: Deming
Quartz New Mexico: Deming
Selenite needles Missouri: Alexandria
Sphalerite Missouri: Alexandria

Gold (*) Alaska: Fairbanks (3); Arizona: Apache Junction, Goldfield; California: Angels Camp (GS), Coloma, Columbia, Jackson, Mariposa, Nevada City, Pine Grove, Placerville; Colorado: Idaho Springs (2); Georgia: Cleveland, Dahlonega (2), Helen; Idaho: Moscow (GS); Indiana: Knightstown; Montana: Alder (O), Helena; North Carolina: Cherokee, Marion, New London, Stanfield, Union Mills; South Dakota: Deadwood, Keystone, Lead

Goshenite Colorado: Lake George

Goyazite Maine: Poland (GS)

Graftonite Maine: Poland (GS); New Hampshire: Grafton (I)

Gummite New Hampshire: Grafton (I)

Gypsum, curved California: Palo Verde (MM)

Hedenburgite New Mexico: Magdalena

Hematite Georgia: Lincolnton; Montana: Helena; New Mexico: Magdalena

Hemimorphite New Mexico: Bingham

Herderite, hydroxyl Maine: Bethel, Poland (GS), West Paris

Herkimer "diamonds" See Quartz

Heterosite Maine: Poland (GS)

Hiddenite (spodumene) North Carolina: Hiddenite

Hureaylite Maine: Poland (GS)

Iron minerals New Mexico: Magdalena

Iron ore Michigan: Iron Mountain (M)

Jade California: Pine Grove

Jadite Montana: Helena (S)

Jahnsite Maine: Poland (GS)

Jasper Arkansas: Murfreesboro (S); California: Pine Grove; Montana: Helena (S); Oklahoma: Kenton; Oregon: Madras, Yachats; Texas: Alpine
   Brown jasper New Mexico: Deming
   Chocolate jasper New Mexico: Deming
   Orange jasper New Mexico: Deming
   Picture jasper Oregon: Mitchell
   Pink jasper New Mexico: Deming
   Variegated jasper New Mexico: Deming
   Yellow jasper New Mexico: Deming

Jarosite Georgia: Lincolnton; New Mexico: Bingham

Kaolinite Maine: Poland (GS)

Kasolite New Hampshire: Grafton (I)

Kosnarite Maine: Poland (GS)

Kyanite Georgia: Lincolnton; North Carolina (*): Franklin, Little Switzerland

Labradorite Texas: Alpine

Lake County "diamonds" See Quartz

Landsite Maine: Poland (GS)

Laueite Maine: Poland (GS)

Lazulite Georgia: Lincolnton

Lepidolite Maine: Poland (GS), West Paris; New Mexico: Dixon; North Carolina (*): Little Switzerland
   Lemon Yellow Lepidolite New Hampshire: Grafton (I)

Lepidomelane New Hampshire: Grafton (I)

Linarite New Mexico: Bingham

Lithiophyllite Maine: Poland (GS); New Hampshire: Grafton (I)

Lollingite Maine: Poland (GS)

Ludlamite Maine: Poland (GS)

Magnesium oxide See Psilomellane

Magnesium oxide minerals New Mexico: Deming

Malachite New Mexico: Magdalena; Utah: Moab (GS)

Manganapatite New Hampshire: Grafton (I)

Manganese minerals New Mexico: Deming

Manganese oxide minerals New Mexico: Deming

Marcasite New Hampshire: Grafton (I)

McCrillisite Maine: Poland (GS)

Mica Maine: Poland (GS), West Paris; New Hampshire: Grafton (I); South Dakota: Custer (GS); Virginia: Amelia

Microcline Maine: Poland (GS)

Microlite New Mexico: Dixon

Mitridatite Maine: Poland (GS)

Molybdenite New Hampshire: Grafton

Montebrasite Maine: Poland (GS)

Montmorillonite Maine: Poland (GS), West Paris; New Hampshire: Grafton (I)

Monzaite Maine: Poland (GS)

Moonstone North Carolina (*): Franklin (7), Little Switzerland, Marion, Spruce Pine

Moraesite Maine: Poland (GS)

Murdochite New Mexico: Bingham

Muscovite Georgia: Lincolnton; New Hampshire: Grafton (I); New Mexico: Dixon

Olivine North Carolina: Spruce Pine

Opal
    Black opal Nevada: Orovado
    Common opal New Mexico: Deming
    Fire opal Nevada: Gerlach, Orovado
    Hyalite opal Maine: Bethel
    Precious opal Idaho: Spencer; Texas: Alpine
    Wood opal Nevada: Denio

Orthoclase Maine: Poland (GS)

Perhamite Maine: Poland (GS)

Parsonite New Hampshire: Grafton (I)

Perlite (black to gray) New Mexico: Deming

Peridot Arkansas: Murfreesboro (S); North Carolina (*): Franklin

Petalite Maine: Poland (GS), West Paris

Phenakite Virginia: Amelia

Phosphosiderite Georgia: Lincolnton; Maine: Poland (GS)

Phosphouranylite Maine: Poland (GS)

Phosphyanylite New Hampshire: Grafton (I)

Pitch Stone with seams of red & brown New Mexico: Deming

Plattnerite New Mexico: Bingham

Pollucite Maine: Poland (GS), West Paris

Psilomelane New Hampshire: Grafton (I)

Purpurite Maine: Poland (GS); New Hampshire: Grafton (I)

Pyrite Georgia: Lincolnton; Maine: Bethel, Poland (GS); New Hampshire: Grafton (I); New Mexico: Magdalena; Tennessee: Ducktown; Virginia: Amelia; Washington: Ravensdale (GS)

Pyrophyllite Georgia: Lincolnton

Pyrrhotite New Hampshire: Grafton (I); Tennessee: Ducktown

Quartz Arkansas: Hot Springs, Jessieville, Mt. Ida (7) (Y), Murfreesboro (S), Paron; California: Pine Grove; Colorado: Lake George; Georgia: Lincolnton; Maine: Poland (GS); Montana: Dillon, Helena (S); New Hampshire: Grafton; New Mexico: Bingham, Deming, Dixon, Socorro (Y); Texas: Alpine; Virginia: Amelia; Washington: Ravensdale (GS)

Blue Georgia: Lincolnton; North Carolina: Marion
Clear North Carolina (*): Franklin, Hiddenite, Little Switzerland, Marion, Spruce Pine
Milky Maine: Bethel
Orange Maine: West Paris
Parallel growth Maine: West Paris
Pseudocubic crystals Maine: West Paris
Rose Georgia: Helen (SA); Maine: Albany, West Paris; New Hampshire: Grafton (I); North Carolina (*): Franklin, Little Switzerland, Marion
Rose (gem quality) Maine: West Paris
Rutilated North Carolina (*): Little Switzerland, Spruce Pine
Smoky Georgia: Helen (SA); Maine: Bethel, West Paris; New Hampshire: Grafton (I); North Carolina (*): Almond, Cherokee, Franklin (6), Hiddenite, Little Switzerland (2), Marion, Spruce Pine (2)
Smoky (gem quality) Maine: West Paris

Quartz "diamonds"
Lake Co. "diamonds" (moon tears) California: Lake County
Cape May "diamonds" New Jersey: Cape May
Herkimer "diamonds" New York: Herkimer, Little Falls, Middleville, St. Johnsville

Reddingite Maine: Poland (GS); New Hampshire: Grafton (I)

Rhodochrosite Maine: Poland (GS)

Rhodolite (garnet) North Carolina: Franklin (2)

Rochbridgeite Maine: Poland (GS)

Rose rocks See Barite Rose

Rubies California: Pine Grove; Georgia: Cleveland, Dahlonega (SA); Montana: Helena (R); North Carolina (*): Almond, Cherokee, Franklin (13), Little Switzerland (2), Spruce Pine (3)

Rutile Georgia: Lincolnton; Maine: Bethel, Poland (GS); North Carolina: Franklin (2), Hiddenite; Virginia: Amelia

Safflorite New Hampshire: Grafton (I)

Sapphires Georgia: Cleveland, Dahlonega (SA); Montana: Alder (O), Clinton (GS), Gem Mountain, Hamilton, Helena (2), Philipsburg; North Carolina (*): Almond, Canton, Cherokee, Franklin (13), Hiddenite, Little Switzerland (2), Spruce Pine

Scheelite Maine: West Paris

Selenite crystals New Mexico: Bingham; Oklahoma: Jet (Y)

Serpentine Montana: Helena (S)

Siderite Maine: Bethel

Silica minerals New Mexico: Deming

Sillimanite New Hampshire: Grafton (I); North Carolina (*): Franklin (2), Hiddenite

Smithsonite New Mexico: Bingham, Magdalena, Socorro (Y)

Spangolite New Mexico: Bingham

Spessartine New Mexico: Dixon

Spodumene Maine: Poland (GS), West Paris; New Mexico: Dixon
    Altered Spodumene Maine: West Paris
    Hiddenite North Carolina: Hiddenite

Staurolite New Hampshire: Grafton (I); Virginia: Stuart

Stewartite Maine: Poland (GS)

Strengite Georgia: Lincolnton

Strunzite Maine: Poland (GS)

Sulfur Georgia: Lincolnton

Switzerite Maine: Poland (GS)

Tantalite-Columbite New Mexico: Dixon; Virginia: Amelia

Thulite North Carolina: Spruce Pine

Thundereggs New Mexico: Deming; Oregon: Madras, Mitchell

Tobernite New Hampshire: Grafton (I)

Topaz Georgia: Cleveland, Helen (SA); Maine: Poland (GS); Montana: Helena (R); New Hampshire: Grafton (I); North Carolina (SA): Cherokee, Franklin (6), Little Switzerland (3), Spruce Pine (3); Texas: Mason (2); Virginia: Amelia
    Blue topaz Colorado: Lake George
    Blue/sherry bicolor Colorado: Lake George
    Phenakite crystals in topaz Colorado: Lake George (U)
    Pink topaz Washington: Ravensdale (GS)
    Sherry topaz Colorado: Lake George

Torberite Maine: Poland (GS)

Tourmaline Maine: Poland (GS), West Paris; North Carolina (*): Franklin (7), Hiddenite, Little Switzerland (3), Spruce Pine (3) (FT); Virginia: Amelia
  Black tourmaline Maine: Albany, Bethel, Poland (GS), West Paris; New Hampshire: Grafton (I)
  Gem tourmaline Maine: West Paris
  Green tourmaline Maine: West Paris
Triphyllite Maine: Poland (GS), West Paris; New Hampshire: Grafton (I)
Triplite Maine: Poland (GS)
Uralolite Maine: Poland (GS)
Uranite Maine: Poland (GS); New Hampshire: Grafton (I) (Species with gummite—world-famous)
Uranium minerals New Hampshire: Grafton (I)
Uranophane New Hampshire: Grafton (I)
Vandendriesscheite New Hampshire: Grafton (I)
Variscite Georgia: Lincolnton
Vesuvianite Maine: Poland (GS), West Paris (2)
Vivianite New Hampshire: Grafton (I)
Voelerkenite New Hampshire: Grafton (I)
Wardilite Maine: Poland (GS)
Whitlockite Maine: Poland (GS)
Whitmoreite Maine: Poland (GS)
Wodginite Maine: Poland (GS)
Wulfenite New Mexico: Bingham
Zircon Maine: Bethel, Poland (GS), West Paris; New Hampshire: Grafton (I)

Annual Events

JANUARY

Quartzite, AZ, Gem and Mineral Shows—Mid-January–mid-February

FEBRUARY

Tucson, AZ, Gem and Mineral Show—First two weeks in February

MARCH

Scottsdale, AZ, Minerals of Arizona Symposium—1 day in March each year, sponsored by the Arizona Mineral & Mining Museum Foundation and the Arizona Department of Mines & Mineral Resources

Boron, CA, Rock Bonanza—Weekend before Easter

APRIL

Alpine, TX, Alpine Gem Show—Mid-April

MAY

Cherokee, OK, The Crystal Festival and Selenite Crystal Dig—First Saturday in May

Noble, OK, Rose Rock Festival—First Saturday in May

Augusta, ME, Maine Mineral Symposium—Third weekend in May

University Park, PA, Mineral Symposium c/o Penn State Mineral Museum—3 days in May

JUNE

Prineville, OR, Rockhounds Pow-Wow—Mid-June

Casper, WY, Tate Geological Museum Symposium on Wyoming Geology

JULY

Franklin, NC, Macon County Gemboree—Third weekend in July

Cottage Grove, OR, Bohemia Mining Days—Four days in July

AUGUST

Spruce Pine, NC, Original North Carolina Mineral and Gem Festival—Four days at the beginning of August

Pittsburgh, PA, Carnegie Museum of Natural History Gem and Mineral Show—Last weekend in August

SEPTEMBER

No information available.

OCTOBER

Coloma, CA, Marshall Gold Discovery State Park Gold Rush Days—End of September–beginning of October

Dahlonega, GA, Gold Rush Days—Third weekend in October

Jasper, GA, Pickens County Marble Festival—First weekend in October

Mt. Ida, AR, Quartz Crystal Festival and World Championship Dig—Second weekend in October

Franklin, NC, "Leaf Looker" Gemboree—Second weekend in October

NOVEMBER

Socorro, NM, New Mexico Mineral Symposium—Two days in November

DECEMBER

No information available.

State Gem and Mineral Symbols

STATE	GEMSTONE	MINERAL	STONE/ROCK
Alabama	Star Blue Quartz (1990)	Hematite (1967)	Marble (1969)
Alaska	Jade (1968)	Gold (1968)	
Arizona	Turquoise (1974)		
Arkansas	Diamond	Quartz	Bauxite
California	Benitoite	Gold	Serpentine (1965)
Colorado	Aquamarine (1971)		
Connecticut	Garnet (1977)		
Delaware		Sillimanite	
Florida	Moonstone		Agatized coral
Georgia	Quartz	Staurolite	
Hawaii	Black Coral		
Idaho	Star Garnet (1967)		
Illinois		Fluorite (1965)	
Indiana			Limestone
Iowa			Geode
Kansas			
Kentucky	Freshwater Pearl		
Louisiana	Agate		
Maine		Tourmaline (1971)	
Maryland			
Massachusetts	Rhodonite	Babingtonite	Plymouth Rock, Dighton Rock, Roxbury Conglomerate
Michigan	Isle Royal Greenstone (Chlorostrolite) (1972)		Petosky Stone (1965)
Minnesota	Lake Superior Agate		
Mississippi			Petrified Wood (1976)
Missouri		Galena (1967)	Mozarkite (1967)
Montana			Sapphire & Agate (1969)
Nebraska	Blue Agate (1967)		Prairie Agate (1967)

STATE	GEMSTONE	MINERAL	STONE/ROCK
Nevada	Virgin Valley Blackfire Opal (1987) (Precious) Turquoise (1987) (Semiprecious)	Silver	Sandstone (1987)
New Hampshire	Smoky Quartz	Beryl	Granite
New Jersey			
New Mexico	Turquoise (1967)		
New York	Garnet (1969)		
North Carolina	Emerald (1973)		
North Dakota			
Ohio	Flint (1965)		
Oklahoma			Barite Rose
Oregon	Sunstone (1987)		Thundereggs (1965)
Pennsylvania			
Rhode Island	Bowenite		Cumberlandite
South Carolina	Amethyst		Blue Granite
South Dakota	Fairburn Agate (1966)	Rose Quartz (1966) (Mineral/Stone)	
Tennessee	Tennessee River Pearls		Limestone and Tennessee Marble
Texas	Texas Blue Topaz (1969) Lone Star Cut (1977) (Gemstone Cut)		Petrified Palmwood (1960)
Utah	Topaz		
Vermont			
Virginia			
Washington	Petrified Wood (1975)		
West Virginia			
Wisconsin		Galena (1971)	Red Granite (1971)
Wyoming	Nephrite Jade (1967)		

Finding Your Own Birthstone

Following is a listing of fee dig sites presented in this four-volume guide where you can find your birthstone! Refer to the individual mine listings for more information on individual mines.

Garnet (January Birthstone) Georgia: Dahlonega (SA), Helen (SA); Idaho: St. Maries; Maine: Albany, Bethel, Poland (GS), West Paris (3); Montana: Alder, Helena (S); New Hampshire: Grafton (I); New Mexico: Dixon; New York: North River; North Carolina (*): Almond, Cherokee, Franklin (7), Hiddenite, Little Switzerland (2), Spruce Pine (3) (FT); Nevada: Ely; Washington: Ravensdale (GS)
  Almandine garnets Maine: Poland (GS); Nevada: Ely
  Pyrope garnets North Carolina: Franklin
  Rhodolite garnets North Carolina: Franklin (5)

Amethyst (February Birthstone) Arkansas: Murfreesboro(S); Georgia: Cleveland, Helen (SA); Maine: Bethel (R), West Paris; Montana: Dillon; Nevada: Sun Valley (GS) (crystal scepters); New Hampshire: Grafton (I); New Mexico: Bingham; North Carolina (*): Cherokee, Franklin (5), Little Switzerland, Spruce Pine (3)

Aquamarine or Bloodstone (March Birthstone):
Aquamarine Maine: Bethel, Poland (GS); New Hampshire: Grafton (I); North Carolina (*): Hiddenite, Little Switzerland (5), Marion, Spruce Pine (2) (FT)
  Brushy Creek Aq. North Carolina: Spruce Pine (FT)
  Weisman Aq. North Carolina: Spruce Pine (FT)
Bloodstone No listing

Diamond (April Birthstone) Arkansas: Murfreesboro

Emerald (May Birthstone) Georgia: Cleveland, Dahlonega (SA); North Carolina (*): Cherokee, Franklin, Hiddenite, Little Switzerland (2), Marion, Spruce Pine (2)
Crabtree Emerald North Carolina: Spruce Pine

Moonstone or Pearl (June Birthstone):
Moonstone North Carolina (*): Franklin (7), Little Switzerland, Marion, Spruce Pine
Pearl No listing

Ruby (July Birthstone) Georgia: Cleveland, Dahlonega (SA); Montana: Helena (R); North Carolina (*): Cherokee, Franklin (13), Little Switzerland (2), Spruce Pine (3)

Peridot or Sardonyx (August Birthstone):
Peridot Arkansas: Murfreesboro (S); North Carolina (*): Franklin
Sardonyx No listing

Sapphire (September Birthstone) Georgia: Dahlonega (SA); Montana: Alder (O), Clinton (GS), Gem Mountian, Hamilton, Helena (2), Philipsburg; North Carolina (*): Canton, Cherokee, Franklin (13), Hiddenite, Little Switzerland (2), Spruce Pine

Opal or Tourmaline (October Birthstone):
Opal
    Black opal Nevada: Orovado
    Common opal New Mexico: Deming
    Fire opal Nevada: Gerlach, Orovado
    Hyalite opal Maine: Bethel
    Precious opal Idaho: Spencer; Texas: Alpine
    Wood opal Nevada: Denio
Tourmaline Maine: Poland (GS), West Paris; North Carolina (*): Franklin (7), Hiddenite, Little Switzerland (3), Spruce Pine (3) (FT); Virginia: Amelia
    Black tourmaline Maine: Albany, Bethel, Poland (GS), West Paris; New Hampshire: Grafton (I)
    Gem tourmaline Maine: West Paris
    Green tourmaline Maine: West Paris

Topaz (November Birthstone) Georgia: Cleveland, Helen (SA); Maine: Poland (GS); Montana: Helena (R); New Hampshire: Grafton (I); North Carolina (SA): Cherokee, Franklin (6), Little Switzerland (3), Spruce Pine (3); Texas: Mason (2); Virginia: Amelia
    Blue topaz Colorado: Lake George
    Blue/sherry bicolor Colorado: Lake George
    Phenakitite in topaz crystals Colorado: Lake George (U)
    Pink topaz Washington: Ravensdale (GS)
    Sherry topaz Colorado: Lake George

Turquoise or Lapis Lazuli (December Birthstone):
Turquoise No listing
Lapis Lazuli No listing

The preceding list of birthstones is taken from a list adopted in 1912 by the American National Association of Jewelers ("The Evolution of Birthstones" from *Jewelry & Gems—The Buying Guide* by Antoinette Matlins and A. C. Bonanno; Gemstone Press, 2001).

Finding Your Anniversary Stone

The following is a listing of fee dig sites contained in this four-volume guide where you can find the stone that is associated with a particular anniversary.

First: Gold (Jewelry) Alaska: Fairbanks (3); Arizona: Goldfield; California: Angels Camp (GS), Coloma, Columbia, Jackson, Mariposa, Nevada City, Pine Grove, Placerville; Colorado: Idaho Springs (2); Georgia: Cleveland, Dahlonega (2), Helen; Idaho: Moscow (GS); Indiana: Knightstown; Montana: Alder (O), Helena; North Carolina: Cherokee, Marion, New London, Stanfield, Union Mills; South Dakota: Deadwood, Keystone, Lead

Second: Garnet Georgia: Dahlonega (SA), Helen (SA); Idaho: St. Maries; Maine: Albany, Bethel, Poland (GS), West Paris (3); Montana: Alder, Helena (S); New Hampshire: Grafton (I); New Mexico: Dixon; New York: North River; North Carolina (*): Almond, Cherokee, Franklin (7), Hiddenite, Little Switzerland (2), Spruce Pine (3) (FT); Nevada: Ely; Washington: Ravensdale (GS)
Almandine garnets Maine: Poland (GS); Nevada: Ely
Pyrope garnets North Carolina: Franklin
Rhodolite garnets North Carolina: Franklin (5)

Third: Pearl No listing

Fourth: Blue Topaz Colorado: Lake George

Fifth: Sapphire Georgia: Cleveland, Dahlonega (SA); Montana: Alder (O), Clinton (GS), Gem Mountain, Hamilton, Helena (2), Philipsburg; North Carolina (*): Almond, Canton, Cherokee, Franklin (13), Hiddenite, Little Switzerland (2), Spruce Pine

Sixth: Amethyst Arkansas: Murfreesboro (S); Georgia: Cleveland, Helen (SA); Maine: Bethel (R), West Paris; Montana: Dillon; Nevada: Sun Valley (GS) (crystal scepters); New Hampshire: Grafton (I); New Mexico: Bingham; North Carolina (*): Cherokee, Franklin (5), Little Switzerland, Spruce Pine (3)

Seventh: Onyx No listing

Eighth: Tourmaline Maine: Poland (GS), West Paris; North Carolina (*): Franklin (7), Hiddenite, Little Switzerland (3), Spruce Pine (3) (FT); Virginia: Amelia
Black tourmaline Maine: Albany, Bethel, Poland (GS), West Paris; New Hampshire: Grafton (I)
Gem tourmaline Maine: West Paris
Green tourmaline Maine: West Paris

Ninth: Lapis Lazuli No listing

Tenth: Diamond (Jewelry) Arkansas: Murfreesboro

Eleventh: Turquoise No listing

Twelfth: Jade No listing

Thirteenth: Citrine Georgia: Helen (SA); North Carolina (SA): Almond, Cherokee, Franklin (5), Little Switzerland, Spruce Pine (3)

Fourteenth: Opal
Black opal Nevada: Orovado
Common opal New Mexico: Deming
Fire opal Nevada: Gerlach, Orovado
Hyalite opal Maine: Bethel
Precious opal Idaho: Spencer; Texas: Alpine
Wood opal Nevada: Denio

Fifteenth: Ruby California: Pine Grove; Georgia: Cleveland, Dahlonega (SA); Montana: Helena (R); North Carolina (*): Almond, Cherokee, Franklin (13), Little Switzerland (2), Spruce Pine (3)

Twentieth: Emerald Georgia: Cleveland, Dahlonega (SA); North Carolina (*): Cherokee, Franklin (1), Hiddenite, Little Switzerland (4), Marion, Spruce Pine (2) (also crabtree emerald)

Twenty-fifth: Silver No listing

Thirtieth: Pearl No listing

Thirty-fifth: Emerald Georgia: Cleveland, Dahlonega (SA); North Carolina (*): Cherokee, Franklin, Hiddenite, Little Switzerland (2), Marion, Spruce Pine (2) (also crabree emerald)

Fortieth: Ruby California: Pine Grove; Georgia: Cleveland, Dahlonega (SA); Montana: Helena (R); North Carolina (*): Almond, Cherokee, Franklin (13), Little Switzerland (2), Spruce Pine (3)

Forty-fifth: Sapphire Georgia: Cleveland, Dahlonega (SA); Montana: Alder, Clinton (GS), Gem Mountain, Hamilton, Helena (2), Philipsburg; North Carolina (*): Almond, Canton, Cherokee, Franklin (13), Hiddenite, Little Switzerland (2), Spruce Pine

Fiftieth: Gold Alaska: Fairbanks (3); Arizona: Apache Junction, Goldfield; California: Angels Camp, Coloma, Columbia, Jackson, Mariposa, Nevada City, Pine Grove, Placerville; Colorado: Idaho Springs (2); Georgia: Cleveland, Dahlonega (2), Helen; Idaho: Moscow (GS); Indiana: Knightstown; Montana: Alder (O), Helena; North Carolina: Cherokee, Marion, New London, Stanfield, Union Mills; South Dakota: Deadwood, Keystone, Lead

Fifty-fifth: Alexandrite No listing

Sixtieth: Diamond Arkansas: Murfreesboro

Finding Your Zodiac Stone

The following is a listing of fee dig sites contained in this four-volume guide where you can find the stone that is associated with a particular zodiac sign. Refer to the individual mine listings for more information.

Aquarius (January 21–February 21) Garnet Georgia: Dahlonega (SA), Helen (SA); Idaho: St. Maries; Maine: Albany, Bethel, Poland (GS), West Paris (3); Montana: Alder, Helena (S); New Hampshire: Grafton (I); New Mexico: Dixon; New York: North River; North Carolina (*): Almond, Cherokee, Franklin (7), Hiddenite, Little Switzerland (2), Spruce Pine (3) (FT); Nevada: Ely; Washington: Ravensdale (GS)
Almandine garnets Maine: Poland (GS); Nevada: Ely
Pyrope garnets North Carolina: Franklin
Rhodolite garnets North Carolina: Franklin (5)

Pisces (February 22–March 21) Amethyst Arkansas: Murfreesboro (S); Georgia: Cleveland, Helen (SA); Maine: Albany, Bethel (R), West Paris; Montana: Dillon; Nevada: Sun Valley (GS) (crystal scepters); New Hampshire: Grafton (I); New Mexico: Bingham; New York: North River; North Carolina (*): Almond, Cherokee, Franklin (5), Little Switzerland, Marion, Spruce Pine (3)

Aries (March 21–April 20) Bloodstone (green chalcedony with red spots) No listing

Taurus (April 21–May 21) Sapphire Georgia: Cleveland, Dahlonega (SA); Montana: Alder (O), Clinton (GS), Gem Mountain, Hamilton, Helena (2), Philipsburg; North Carolina (*): Almond, Canton, Cherokee, Franklin (13), Hiddenite, Little Switzerland (2), Spruce Pine

Gemini (May 22–June 21) Agate Arkansas: Murfreesboro(S); Iowa: Bonaporte; Montana: Helena (S); Nevada: Gerlach; New Mexico: Deming (GS); Oklahoma: Kenton (2); Oregon: Yachats; South Dakota: Wall; Texas: Three Rivers; Virginia: Amelia
Banded agate Texas: Alpine
Fire agate California: Palo Verde
Iris agate Texas: Alpine
Ledge agate Oregon: Madras
Moss agate Oregon: Madras, Mitchell; Texas: Alpine (2), Wyoming: Shell
Polka-dot jasp-agate Oregon: Madras
Plume agate Oregon: Madras
Pompom agate Texas: Alpine
Rainbow agate Oregon: Madras
Red plume agate Texas: Alpine

Cancer (June 22–July 22) Emerald Georgia: Cleveland, Dahlonega (SA); North Carolina (*): Cherokee, Franklin, Hiddenite, Little Switzerland (2), Spruce Pine (2)

Crabtree emerald North Carolina: Spruce Pine

Leo (July 23–August 22) Onyx No listing

Virgo (August 23–September 22) Carnelian No listing

Libra (September 23–October 23) Chrysolite or Peridot:
Peridot Arkansas: Murfreesboro (S); North Carolina (*): Franklin

Scorpio (October 24–November 21) Beryl Maine: Albany, Poland (GS), West Paris; New Mexico: Dixon; North Carolina (*): Little Switzerland (2), Spruce Pine (2); Virginia: Amelia (2)
    Aqua beryl New Hampshire: Grafton (I)
    Blue beryl New Hampshire: Grafton (I)
    Golden beryl North Carolina: Spruce Pine (FT); New Hampshire: Grafton (I)

Sagittarius (November 22–December 21) Topaz Georgia: Cleveland, Helen (SA); Maine: Poland (GS); Montana: Helena (R); New Hampshire: Grafton (I); North Carolina (SA): Cherokee, Franklin (6), Little Switzerland (3), Spruce Pine (3); Texas: Mason (2); Virginia: Amelia
    Blue topaz Colorado: Lake George
    Blue/sherry bicolor Colorado: Lake George
    Phenakitite crystals in topaz Colorado: Lake George (U)
    Pink topaz Washington: Ravensdale (GS)
    Sherry topaz Colorado: Lake George

Capricorn (December 22–January 21) Ruby California: Pine Grove; Georgia: Cleveland, Dahlonega (SA); Montana: Helena (R); North Carolina (*): Almond, Cherokee, Franklin (13), Little Switzerland (2), Spruce Pine (3)

The preceding list of zodiacal stones has been passed on from an early Hindu legend (taken from *Jewelry & Gems—The Buying Guide* by Antoinette Matlins and A. C. Bonanno, Gemstone Press, 2001).

The following is an old Spanish list, probably representing Arab traditions, which ascribes the following stones to various signs of the zodiac (taken from *Jewelry & Gems—The Buying Guide* by Antoinette Matlins and A. C. Bonanno, Gemstone Press, 2001).

Aquarius (January 21–February 21) Amethyst Arkansas: Murfreesboro (S); Georgia: Cleveland, Helen (SA); Maine: Bethel (R), West Paris; Montana: Dillon; New Hampshire: Grafton (I); New Mexico: Bingham; North Carolina (*): Almond, Cherokee, Franklin (5), Little Switzerland, Marion, Spruce Pine (3)
Crystal scepters Nevada: Sun Valley (GS)

Pisces (February 22–March 21) Undistinguishable

Aries (March 21–April 20) Quartz Arkansas: Hot Springs, Jessieville, Mt. Ida (7) (Y), Murfreesboro (S), Paron; California: Pine Grove; Colorado: Lake George; Maine: Poland (GS); Montana: Dillon, Helena; New Hampshire: Grafton; New Mexico: Bingham, Deming, Dixon, Socorro (Y); Texas: Alpine; Virginia: Amelia; Washington: Ravensdale (GS)
Blue Georgia: Lincolnton; North Carolina: Marion
Clear North Carolina (*): Franklin, Hiddenite, Little Switzerland, Marion, Spruce Pine
Milky Maine: Bethel
Orange Maine: West Paris
Parallel growth Maine: West Paris
Pseudocubic crystals Maine: West Paris
Rose Georgia: Helen (SA); Maine: Albany, West Paris; New Hampshire: Grafton (I); North Carolina (*): Franklin, Little Switzerland, Marion
Rose (gem quality) Maine: Albany, West Paris
Rutilated North Carolina (*): Little Switzerland, Spruce Pine
Smoky Georgia: Helen (SA); Maine: Bethel, West Paris; New Hampshire: Grafton (I); North Carolina (*): Almond, Cherokee, Franklin (6), Hiddenite, Little Switzerland (2), Marion, Spruce Pine (2)
Smoky (gem quality) Maine: West Paris

Quartz "diamonds"
Lake Co. "diamonds" (moon tears) California: Lake County
Cape May "diamonds" New Jersey: Cape May
Herkimer "diamonds" New York: Herkimer, Little Falls, Middleville, St. Johnsville

Taurus (April 21–May 21) Rubies, Diamonds:
Rubies California: Pine Grove; Georgia: Dahlonega (SA); Montana: Helena (R); North Carolina (*): Almond, Cherokee, Franklin (13), Little Switzerland (2), Spruce Pine (3)
Diamonds Arkansas: Murfreesboro

Gemini (May 22–June 21) Sapphire Georgia: Cleveland, Dahlonega (SA); Montana: Alder (O), Clinton (GS), Gem Mountain, Hamilton, Helena (2), Philipsburg; North Carolina (*): Almond, Canton, Cherokee, Franklin (13), Hiddenite, Little Switzerland (2), Spruce Pine

Cancer (June 22–July 22) Agate and Beryl:
Agate Arkansas: Murfreesboro (S); Iowa: Bonaporte; Montana: Helena (S); Nevada: Gerlach; New Mexico: Deming (GS); Oklahoma: Kenton (2); Oregon: Yachats; South Dakota: Wall; Texas: Three Rivers; Virginia: Amelia
Banded agate Texas: Alpine
Fire agate California: Palo Verde
Iris agate Texas: Alpine
Ledge agate Oregon: Madras
Moss agate Oregon: Madras, Mitchell; Texas: Alpine (2), Wyoming: Shell
Polka-dot agate Oregon: Madras (R)

Plume agate Oregon: Madras
Pompom agate Texas: Alpine
Rainbow agate Oregon: Madras (R)
Red plume agate Texas: Alpine

Beryl Maine: Albany, Poland (GS), West Paris; New Mexico, Dixon; North Carolina (*): Little Switzerland (2), Spruce Pine (2); Virginia: Amelia (2)
Aqua beryl New Hampshire: Grafton (I)
Blue beryl New Hampshire: Grafton (I)
Golden beryl North Carolina: Spruce Pine (FT); New Hampshire: Grafton (I)

Leo (July 23–August 22) Topaz Georgia: Cleveland, Helen (SA); Maine: Poland (GS); Montana: Helena (R); New Hampshire: Grafton (I); North Carolina (SA): Cherokee, Franklin (6), Little Switzerland (3), Spruce Pine (3); Texas: Mason (2); Virginia: Amelia
Blue topaz Colorado: Lake George
Blue/sherry bicolor Colorado: Lake George
Phenakitite crystals in topaz Colorado: Lake George (U)
Pink topaz Washington: Ravensdale (GS)
Sherry topaz Colorado: Lake George

Virgo (August 23–September 22) Bloodstone (green chalcedony with red spots)
No listing

Libra (September 23–October 23) Jasper Arkansas: Murfreesboro (S); California: Pine Grove; Montana: Helena; Oklahoma: Kenton; Oregon: Madras, Yachats; Texas: Alpine
Brown jasper New Mexico: Deming
Chocolate jasper New Mexico: Deming
Orange jasper New Mexico: Deming
Picture jasper Oregon: Mitchell
Pink jasper New Mexico: Deming
Variegated jasper New Mexico: Deming
Yellow jasper New Mexico: Deming

Scorpio (October 24–November 21) Garnet Georgia: Dahlonega (SA), Helen (SA); Idaho: St. Maries; Maine: Albany, Bethel, Poland (GS), West Paris (3); Montana: Alder, Helena (S); New Hampshire: Grafton (I); New Mexico: Dixon; North Carolina (*): Almond, Cherokee, Franklin (7), Hiddenite, Little Switzerland (2), Spruce Pine (3) (FT); Nevada: Ely; Washington: Ravensdale (GS)
Almandine garnets Maine: Poland (GS); Nevada: Ely
Pyrope garnets North Carolina: Franklin
Rhodolite garnets North Carolina: Franklin (5)

Sagittarius (November 22–December 21) Emerald Georgia: Cleveland, Dahlonega (SA); North Carolina (*): Cherokee, Franklin, Hiddenite, Little Switzerland (2), Marion, Spruce Pine (2)
Crabtree emerald North Carolina: Spruce Pine

Capricorn (December 22–January 21) Chalcedony New Mexico: Deming
Blue chalcedony Nevada: Sun Valley (GS)

Some Publications on Gems and Minerals

Lapidary Journal

Subscriptions
P.O. Box 56553
Boulder, CO 80322
(800) 676-4336
www.lapidaryjournal.com

Rocks & Minerals

5341 Thrasher Dr.
Cincinnati, OH 45247
Phone: (800) 365-9753
Fax: (202) 293-6130
www.mineralart.com/rocks_and_
minerals

Rock & Gem

c/o Miller Magazines, Inc.
4880 Market Street
Ventura, CA 93003-7783
Phone: (805) 644-3824
www.rockngem.com

Gold Prospector

Gold Prospectors Association of America, Inc.
P.O. Box 891509
Temecula, CA 92589
Phone: (909) 699-4749
www.goldprospectors.org

Send Us Your Feedback

Disclaimer

The authors have made every reasonable effort to obtain accurate information for this guide. However, much of the information in the book is based on material provided by the sites and has not been verified independently. The information given here does not represent recommendations, but merely a listing of information. The authors and publisher accept no liability for any accident or loss incurred when readers are patronizing the establishments listed herein. The authors and publisher accept no liability for errors or omissions. Since sites may shut down or change their hours of operations or fees without advance notice, please call the site before your visit for confirmation before planning your trip.

The authors would appreciate being informed of changes, additions, or deletions that should be made to this guide. To that end, a form is attached, which can be filled out and mailed to the authors for use in future editions of the guide.

Have We Missed Your Mine or Museum?

This is a project with a national scope, based on extensive literature search, phone and mail inquiry, and personal investigation. However, we are dealing with a business in which many owners are retiring or closing and selling their sites. In addition, many of the mines, guide services, and smaller museums have limited publicity, known more by word of mouth than by publication. Thus, it is possible that your operation or one you have visited was not included in this guide. Please let us know if you own or operate a mine, guide service, or museum, or have visited a mine, guide service, or museum that is not in the guide. It will be considered for inclusion in the next edition of the guide. Send updates to:

Treasure Hunter's Guides
GemStone Press
Route 4, Sunset Farm Offices
P.O. Box 237
Woodstock, VT 05091

Do You Have a Rockhounding Story to Share?

If you have a special story about a favorite dig site, send it in for consideration for use in the next edition of the guide.

A Request to Mines and Museums:

For sites already included in this guide, we request that you put us on your annual mailing list so that we may have an updated copy of your information.

Notes on Museums

In this guide we have included listings of museums with noteworthy gem, mineral, or rock collections. We particularly tried to find local museums displaying gems or minerals native to the area where they are located. This list is by no means complete, and if you feel we missed an important listing, let us know by completing the following form. Since these guides focus specifically on gems and minerals, only those exhibits have been recognized in the museum listings, and we do not mention any collection or exhibits of fossils. See our sequel on fossils for information on fossil collections.

READER'S CONTRIBUTION

I would like to supply the following information for possible inclusion in the next edition of *The Treasure Hunter's Guide*:

Type of entry: ☐ fee dig ☐ guide service ☐ museum ☐ mine tour
☐ annual event

This is a: ☐ new entry ☐ entry currently in the guide

Nature of info: ☐ addition ☐ change ☐ deletion

Please describe (brochure and additional info may be attached):

_____

_____

_____

_____

Please supply the following in case we need to contact you regarding your information:

Name: _____

Address: _____

_____

_____

Phone: ( ) _____

E-mail: _____

Date: _____

FIELD NOTES

FIELD NOTES

FIELD NOTES

FIELD NOTES

FIELD NOTES

FIELD NOTES

FIELD NOTES

FIELD NOTES

FIELD NOTES

FIELD NOTES

FIELD NOTES

The "Unofficial Bible" for the Gem & Jewelry Buyer

JEWELRY & GEMS:
THE BUYING GUIDE, 5TH EDITION

*How to Buy Diamonds, Pearls, Colored Gemstones,
Gold & Jewelry with Confidence and Knowledge*

by Antoinette Matlins, P.G., *and* A. C. Bonanno, F.G.A., P.G., A.S.A.

—*over 250,000 copies in print*—

Learn the tricks of the trade from *insiders:* How to buy diamonds, pearls, precious and other popular colored gems with confidence and knowledge. More than just a buying guide . . . discover what's available and what choices you have, what determines quality as well as cost, what questions to ask before you buy and what to get in writing. Easy to read and understand. Excellent for staff training.

6" x 9", 320 pp., 16 full-color pages & over 200 color and b/w illustrations and photos; index
Quality Paperback, ISBN 0-943763-31-2 **$18.95**
Hardcover, ISBN 0-943763-30-4 **$24.95**

• COMPREHENSIVE • EASY TO READ • PRACTICAL •
ENGAGEMENT & WEDDING RINGS, 3RD EDITION

by Antoinette Matlins, P.G., *and* A. C. Bonanno, F.G.A., A.S.A., M.G.A.

Tells **everything you need to know to design, select, buy and enjoy that "perfect" ring** and to truly experience the wonder and excitement that should be part of it.

Updated, expanded, filled with valuable information.

Engagement & Wedding Rings, 3rd Ed., will help you make the *right* choice. You will discover romantic traditions behind engagement and wedding rings, how to select the right style and design for *you,* tricks to get what you want on a budget, ways to add new life to an "heirloom," what to do to protect yourself against fraud, and much more.

Dazzling 16-page color section of rings showing antique to contemporary designs.
Over 400 illustrations and photographs. Index.
6" x 9", 320 pp., Quality Paperback, ISBN 0-943763-41-X **$18.95**

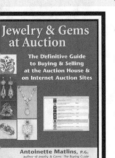

JEWELRY & GEMS AT AUCTION
*The Definitive Guide to Buying & Selling
at the Auction House & on Internet Auction Sites*

by Antoinette Matlins, P.G.

with contributions by Jill Newman

As buying and selling at auctions—both traditional auction houses and "virtual" Internet auctions—moves into the mainstream, **consumers need to know how to "play the game."** There are treasures to be had and money to be saved and made, but buying and selling at auction offers unique risks as well as unique opportunities. This book makes available—for the first time—detailed information on how to buy and sell jewelry and gems at auction without making costly mistakes.

6" x 9", 352 pp., fully illustrated
Quality Paperback Original, ISBN 0-943763-29-0 **$19.95**

FOR CREDIT CARD ORDERS CALL 800-962-4544

Available from your bookstore or directly from the publisher. TRY YOUR BOOKSTORE FIRST.

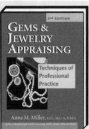

DIAMONDS: THE ANTOINETTE MATLINS BUYING GUIDE

How to Select, Buy, Care for & Enjoy Diamonds with Confidence and Knowledge

by Antoinette Matlins, P.G.

Practical, comprehensive, and easy to understand, this book includes price guides for old and new cuts and for fancy-color, treated, and synthetic diamonds. **Explains in detail** how to read diamond grading reports and offers important advice for after buying a diamond. **The "unofficial bible" for all diamond buyers who want to get the most for their money.**

6" x 9", 220 pp., 12 full-color pages & many b/w illustrations and photos; index
Quality Paperback Original, ISBN 0-943763-32-0 **$16.95**

COLORED GEMSTONES:
THE ANTOINETTE MATLINS BUYING GUIDE

How to Select, Buy, Care for & Enjoy Sapphires, Emeralds, Rubies and Other Colored Gems with Confidence and Knowledge

by Antoinette Matlins, P.G.

This practical, comprehensive, easy-to-understand guide **provides in depth** all the information you need to buy colored gems with confidence. Includes price guides for popular gems, opals, and synthetic stones. Provides examples of gemstone grading reports and offers important advice for after buying a gemstone. **Shows anyone shopping for colored gemstones how to get the most for their money.**

6" x 9", 224 pp., 16 full-color pages & many b/w illustrations and photos; index
Quality Paperback Original, ISBN 0-943763-33-9 **$16.95**

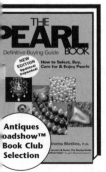

THE PEARL BOOK, 3RD EDITION:
THE DEFINITIVE BUYING GUIDE

How to Select, Buy, Care for & Enjoy Pearls
by Antoinette Matlins, P.G.

COMPREHENSIVE • EASY TO READ • PRACTICAL

This comprehensive, authoritative guide tells readers everything they need to know about pearls to fully understand and appreciate them, and avoid any unexpected—and costly—disappointments, now and in future generations.

- A journey into the rich history and romance surrounding pearls.
- The five factors that determine pearl value & judging pearl quality.
- What to look for, what to look out for: How to spot fakes. Treatments.
- Differences between natural, cultured and imitation pearls, and ways to separate them.
- Comparisons of all types of pearls, in every size and color, from every pearl-producing country.

6" x 9", 232 pp., 16 full-color pages & over 250 color and b/w illustrations and photos; index
Quality Paperback, ISBN 0-943763-35-5 **$19.95**

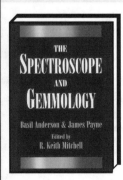

Buy Your *"Tools of the Trade"*...

Gem Identification Instruments directly from *GemStone Press*

Whatever instrument you need, GemStone Press can help.
Use our convenient order form, or contact us directly for assistance.

Complete Pocket Instrument Set
SPECIAL SAVINGS!
BUY THIS ESSENTIAL TRIO AND SAVE 12%
Used together, you can identify 85% of all gems with these three
portable, pocket-sized instruments—the essential trio.
10X Triplet Loupe • Chelsea Filter • Calcite Dichroscope

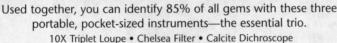

Pocket Instrument Set:
Standard: With Standard 10X Loupe • OPL Dichroscope • Chelsea Filter **only $144.95**
Deluxe: With Bausch & Lomb 10X Loupe • EzVIEW Dichroscope • Chelsea Filter **only $179.95**

ITEM / QUANTITY	PRICE EA.*	TOTAL $
Pocket Instrument Sets		
_____ **Standard:** With Standard 10X Loupe • OPL Dichroscope • Chelsea Filter	$144.95	$ _____
_____ **Deluxe:** With Bausch & Lomb 10X Loupe • EzVIEW Dichroscope • Chelsea Filter	$179.95	_____
Loupes—Professional Jeweler's 10X Triplet Loupes		
_____ Bausch & Lomb 10X Triplet Loupe	$44.00	_____
_____ Standard 10X Triplet Loupe	$29.00	_____
_____ Darkfield Diamond View	$58.95	_____
• Spot filled diamonds, other enhancements and zoning instantly. Operates with large maglite (optional).		
_____ RosGem Loupe-Fillfinder	$69.95	_____
Analyzer		
_____ Gem Analyzer	$285.00	_____
• Combines Darkfield Loupe, Polariscope, and Immersion Cell		
Calcite Dichroscopes		
_____ Dichroscope (EzVIEW)	$115.00	_____
_____ Dichroscope (OPL)	$89.95	_____
Color Filters		
_____ Chelsea Filter	$44.95	_____
_____ Synthetic Emerald Filter Set (Hanneman)	$32.00	_____
_____ Tanzanite Filter (Hanneman)	$28.00	_____
_____ Bead Buyer's & Parcel Picker's Filter Set (Hanneman)	$24.00	_____
Diamond Testers and Tweezers		
_____ SSEF Diamond-Type Spotter	$150.00	_____
_____ Diamondnite Dual Tester	$269.00	_____
_____ Diamond Tweezers/Locking	$10.65	_____
_____ Diamond Tweezers/Non-Locking	$7.80	_____
Jewelry Cleaners		
_____ Ionic Cleaner—Home size model	$69.95	_____
_____ Ionic Solution—16 oz. bottle	$20.00	_____

See Over for More Instruments

Buy Your *"Tools of the Trade..."*

Gem Identification Instruments directly from *GemStone Press*

Whatever instrument you need, GemStone Press can help.
Use our convenient order form, or contact us directly for assistance.

ITEM / QUANTITY	PRICE EA.*	TOTAL $

Lamps—Ultraviolet & High Intensity

_____ Small LW/SW (UVP)	$71.00	_____
_____ Large LW/SW (UVP)	$189.00	_____
_____ Viewing Cabinet for Large Lamp (UVP)	$147.00	_____
_____ **Purchase Large Lamp & Cabinet together**	$299.00	_____
for $299 and save $37.00		
_____ Dialite Flip Lamp (Eickhorst)	$64.95	_____

For Use with the SSEF Diamond-Type Spotter

_____ SSEF High-Intensity Shortwave Lamp	$499.00	_____
_____ Portable SSEF High-Intensity Shortwave Lamp	$300.00	_____

Other Light Sources

_____ Large Maglite	$15.00	_____
_____ Flex Light	$29.95	_____

Refractometers

_____ Standard Refractometer (Eickhorst)	$625.00	_____
_____ Pocket Refractometer (Eickhorst)	$495.00	_____
_____ Refractive Index Liquid 1.81—10 gram	$42.50	_____

Spectroscopes

_____ Spectroscope—Pocket-sized model (OPL)	$89.00	_____
_____ Spectroscope—Desk model w/stand (OPL)	$225.00	_____

Shipping/Insurance per order in the U.S.: $4.95 first item,   SHIPPING/INS. $_____
$3.00 each add'l item; $7.95 total for pocket instrument set.

Outside the U.S.: Please specify *insured* shipping method you prefer
and provide a credit card number for payment.   **TOTAL $ _____** **

Check enclosed for $ _____ (Payable to: GEMSTONE PRESS)
Charge my credit card: ❑ Visa ❑ MasterCard
Name on Card _____
Cardholder Address: Street _____
City/State/Zip _____
Credit Card # _____ Exp. Date _____
Signature _____ Phone (_____)_____
Please send to: ❑ Same as Above ❑ Address Below
Name _____
Street _____
City/State/Zip _____ Phone (_____)_____

Phone, mail, fax, or e-mail orders to:

GEMSTONE PRESS, P.O. Box 237, Woodstock, VT 05091
Tel: (802) 457-4000 • Fax: (802) 457-4004 • Credit Card Orders: (800) 962-4544
sales@gemstonepress.com • www.gemstonepress.com
Generous Discounts on Quantity Orders

See Over for More Instruments

*Prices, manufacturing specifications, and terms subject to change
without notice. Orders accepted subject to availability.
**All orders must be prepaid by credit card, money order or check
in U.S. funds drawn on a U.S. bank.

Please send me:

CAMEOS OLD & NEW, 3RD EDI
_____ copies at $19.95 (Quali

COLORED GEMSTONES: THE ANTOINETTE MATLINS BUYING GUIDE
_____ copies at $16.

DIAMONDS: THE ANTC
_____ copies at $16.

ENGAGEMENT & WED
_____ copies at $18.

GEM IDENTIFICATION
A HANDS-ON GUIDE TO MORE CONFIDENT BUYING & SELLING
_____ copies at $34.95 (Hardcover) *plus s/h**

GEMS & JEWELRY APPRAISING, 2ND EDITION
_____ copies at $39.95 (Hardcover) *plus s/h**

ILLUSTRATED GUIDE TO JEWELRY APPRAISING, 2ND EDITION
_____ copies at $39.95 (Hardcover) *plus s/h**

JEWELRY & GEMS AT AUCTION: THE DEFINITIVE GUIDE TO BUYING & SELLING AT THE AUCTION HOUSE & ON INTERNET AUCTION SITES
_____ copies at $19.95 (Quality Paperback) *plus s/h**

JEWELRY & GEMS: THE BUYING GUIDE, 5TH EDITION
_____ copies at $18.95 (Quality Paperback) *plus s/h**
_____ copies at $24.95 (Hardcover) *plus s/h**

THE PEARL BOOK, 3RD EDITION: THE DEFINITIVE BUYING GUIDE
_____ copies at $19.95 (Quality Paperback) *plus s/h**

THE SPECTROSCOPE AND GEMMOLOGY
_____ copies at $69.95 (Hardcover) *plus s/h**

TREASURE HUNTER'S GEM & MINERAL GUIDES TO THE U.S.A., 2ND EDITIONS:
WHERE & HOW TO DIG, PAN AND MINE YOUR OWN GEMS & MINERALS—
IN 4 REGIONAL VOLUMES $14.95 per copy (Quality Paperback) *plus s/h**
_____ copies of NE States   _____ copies of SE States   _____ copies of NW States   _____ copies of SW State

* In U.S.: Shipping/Handling: $3.75 for 1st book, $2.00 each additional book.
  Outside U.S.: Specify shipping method (insured) and provide a credit card number for payment.

Check enclosed for $_____ (Payable to: GEMSTONE Press)
Charge my credit card: ❑ Visa ❑ MasterCard
Name on Card (PRINT) _____
Cardholder Address: Street _____
City/State/Zip _____ E-mail _____
Credit Card # _____ Exp. Date _____
Signature _____ Phone (____)_____
Please send to: ❑ Same as Above ❑ Address Below
Name (PRINT) _____
Street _____
City/State/Zip _____ Phone (____)_____

Phone, mail, fax, or e-mail orders to:
GEMSTONE PRESS, Sunset Farm Offices,
Rte. 4, P.O. Box 237, Woodstock, VT 05091
Tel: (802) 457-4000 • *Fax:* (802) 457-4004
Credit Card Orders: (800) 962-4544
sales@gemstonepress.com
www.gemstonepress.com
Generous Discounts on Quantity Orders

Prices subject to change

Try Your Bookstore First